Driving
South to
Inverness

Postscript to an active life
by Phoebe Caldwell

Pavilion

Driving South to Inverness

Postscript to an active life

By Phoebe Caldwell

© Pavilion Publishing and Media Ltd

Published by:
Pavilion Publishing and Media Ltd
Rayford House, School Road, Hove, East Sussex, BN3 5HX
Tel: 01273 434 943
Fax: 01273 227 308
Email: info@pavpub.com

Published 2016

ISBN: 978-1-911028-31-4

Author: Phoebe Caldwell
Editor: Mike Benge, Pavilion Publising and Media Ltd
Cover design: Tony Pitt, Pavilion Publishing and Media Ltd, with special thanks to Emily Jones
Layout design: Emma Dawe, Pavilion Publishing and Media Ltd
Printing: Short Run Press

With love to Margaret and Kenny, who stuffed
all my chattels in their van and built enough
shelves in my new flat to accommodate them.

Contents

Where am I?

The title of this book requires some explanation. I am a Southerner. Returning home from working in Orkney, I'm struck by the incongruity of driving south to Inverness, since my internal sat-nav is insisting this granite city lies to the north, somewhere up there beyond the Grampians.

It seemed a good title for a book, having about it the mental twitch that highlights both discontinuity and potential interest – but at the time, lacked context. The theme it has now been co-opted to address is that of displacement and loss of identity in a strange place, and the struggle to achieve a balance between community and individuality as one grows old. Where am I and what do I mean by 'home' and 'self', and what happens when I feel these are threatened?

Driving South to Inverness is in one sense a diary about getting old with its accompanying move from what I regard as home to living in a small flat – 'downsizing' as it is known, a word I dislike since it is clearly a euphemism for shrinkage. I am grateful to a friend who suggests it is better to regard the process as 'editing', which places the emphasis on selection rather than contraction. Either way, one has to get rid of a lot of stuff, treasures, stones, strips of bark, bits of one's life (such as the top ring of an old fire extinguisher pulled out of stinking mud in Sutton Pool, Plymouth Harbour, encrusted with barnacles), without shedding too much of who one feels one is. I did keep this one.

Kenny has a more succinct description: 'It's like trying to launch an oil tanker into a canal'.

The setting for this book is Craven, North Yorkshire, moving from my own home in the Wenning Valley into a sheltered flat in Settle (an adjacent market town on the River Ribble), crossing the great Craven Fault from Bowland, a barren hilly area lolling like a row of basking seals, to the higher crusty hills of the Dales – millstone grit peaks resting on limestone pavement. I've spent the last 40 years working with adults and children with severe autism, using an approach based on responding to an individual's personal body language. As I becomes less mobile, the battle is on as to how long I can continue to contribute to a field which is desperately short of expertise. Perhaps the struggle will be helped if I simplify my domestic arrangements?

In addition to geographical relocation, I notice that I also have a grammatical problem: how to define the distance between myself, writer, and you, reader. Assuming you still wish to continue with this account, a decision has to be made as to the degree of closeness that is mutually agreeable. To put it personally, how much introspection and 'self' can you stand, because if this account is going to mean anything more than a report, self-reflection and closeness is the direction we shall have to take.

Every line crystallises this dilemma: which pronouns shall I draw from the potpourri of possibilities, 'I', 'We' 'You', or the less personal, 'One'? It's not so much about you and me getting too close but rather a struggle against the decoy of self-centredness, flashy feathers dangling from a lure.

The choice represents the degree of intimacy; retreat to the third person is a gauge of emotional sensitivity. So, against the rules I've decided to opt for inconsistency, using whichever suits the affective voice of the paragraph in question.

But first to the physical business of writing. Around the age of five my sister, Prudence, sat me down, produced a pencil and sheet of paper, ruled a set of narrow parallel lines and announced that now I could read it was time for me to learn to write. My fist was clumsy as I struggled to copy the swirls and curlicues of italic script. Loops dangled from the tracks like hairpins trying to escape from my mother's hairnet.

All change: at the age of seven when I was sent to school. My cursive essays were crumpled and thrown into the waste paper basket, 'binned' as we say now. For weeks I sat in front of copy books developing 'good round letters', almost a religion in this Quaker school and certainly deemed to be a measure of my character. The result of this abrupt repackaging is that in adult life my writing is all over the place and sometimes even I hardly recognise it. Coupled with spending my eighth year learning to spell in America, computers came as a relief, although the spell-check rebelled on this particular text and sent me a note saying that there were too many spelling mistakes for it to handle and was shutting down. Fortunately my friend Jo, who is an editor, is more accommodating.

Now that I can pin my thoughts down on paper, a disadvantage of the diary formula is that it is a present happening, told as it occurs; there is no possibility of modification in the light of further developments, nothing in the way of subsequent experience that might allow one to lean on and alter an immediate affective response. So this description of moving into care is in the present and needs to be told how it feels.

In fact, I've never been a good diary keeper, even in the sense of an appointments calendar. The whole idea of chopping time into 24 hour sections seems to me like loose beads – meaningless if not linked by their emotional string. 'I do this today and tomorrow I shall do that', lacks connection between cause and effect.

So, this diarist wobbles between prospect and retrospect. If she sticks to 'to-do', her account is two dimensional, like the inhabitant of Flatland she will lack depth[1]. On the other hand, hindsight opens the door to creative interpretation – which is undoubtedly more fun but carries with it the danger of straying into fiction. And as David Eagleman points out, from the neurobiological point of view, our current memory of our past 'is not a faithful record. Instead it's a reconstruction and sometimes this can border on mythology[2]'. As time moves on our brain is constantly reinterpreting our memories in the light of additional neuronal connections and further experience.

So I can't be absolutely certain whether the 14 year old who inhabits my memory did finally manage to swim across the creek, or whether the picture she has of standing on the far side and looking back across the water to the elm-planked seawall built by her brother is part of a silvery dream tacked on to a wish.

More clearly defined is the day I walked round the oyster bed at low tide. Iodine mud oozed between my toes and rough-edged shells cut into the soles of my bare feet. Until I came to the drain. My legs floundered in slop. Starting to panic, I remembered my father's advice. Characteristically, it was not a prohibition, 'do not walk on the mud', but rather, 'if you ever get stuck, lie down and spread your weight'. Being prone felt counter-intuitive but I stopped sinking and managed to wriggle

---

1   Abbott E (1884) *Flatland: A romance of many dimensions.* Seely & Co

2   Eagleman D (2015) *The Brain: The story of you.* Edinburgh: Canongate Books.

off on my stomach. Plastered black, I staggered home; a true monster from the deep.

Is this a composite memory? Looking back, I should be surprised if an observer on the edge of the marsh told me that I had simply stood on the flint shore and imagined a 'what if...', and this was the basis of my adventure. The smell of the mud overlaid by wafts of sea lavender – and the way that the mud squeezed like black butter curls through the gaps between my toes lend convincing olfactory and haptic support to what I perceive as my authentic version. Nevertheless, since my image of myself relates to retrieval of experiences, it does call into question who and what I am. How much of 'what I believe to be me' is real?

On the other hand, what has happened (or what I recall as having happened) and what has still to happen, are linked through memory; my stories help to predicate my future. Advance warnings such as, 'not everything is as it seems' and 'watch where you put your feet', guide my behaviour, the latter especially useful since the small hairs that inform my balance system are slowly shrivelling: if I lean too far forward, the automatic brake I've come to rely on is no longer applied and I pitch forwards.

But perhaps the fact that I am at least conscious of my brain's tendency to weave together past and present (with an eye on the future), provides an anchor to its desire to drift away into fantasy and fiction.

Where I am now, there's still a battle going on between the survival of 'me' in both the physical and psychological sense. Despite the strictures of my physio and personal dedication to ten minutes a day on an exercise bike, physical fitness is a missed deadline, a concept relating to the past. And psychological survival requires inner resources, which are being tested by the opposing attractions of inertia. The struggle is sharpened by moving into what is in some respect community living – at least there are other people around me, rather than being a totally free agent.

Backwards and forwards: focus on 'self' goes against the grain, since much of my education was devoted to shifting attention away from my own interests to listening and responding to other people's points of view (plus admonitions to avoid the deadly sin of egotism). These were quite explicit: 'you must think about other people and show them you are interested in them when you talk to them'. Why should I? Once, I did not know what this other was that was not me.

It takes time to emerge from seeing others only as they affect oneself to perceiving them as totally separate entities, each with their own lives, their own points of view; a conflict waged against the instinct for satisfying personal need.

Quite a trivial remark can open the door to alternative landscapes. I am sitting next to a young Frenchman, my first foreigner. Out of the blue he says how much better things would have turned out if Elizabeth I had married Philip of Spain. It may seem ridiculous, but momentarily the world of this hitherto conventional adolescent wobbled in its orbit while she struggled with the possibility that another person can have, not only a different point of view, but also operate from an entirely different centre. When I protest that you can't play 'what if...' with history he replies that you can – and it opens the mind to interesting speculation and alternative options.

I am going to have to rewrite the script: the rest of the world is not necessarily about me.

We all shudder at the idea of being 'put in a home'. However justified or not, the image it conjures is of a room full of the demented and incontinent wrapped in the smell of urine and overcooked Savoy cabbage: not a scenario in which any of us wishes to find ourselves a bit player. The alternative is euphemistically known as 'sheltered living', retaining independence within an umbrella of care, a service that picks you up if you fall over and checks daily to see if you are still alive. It also requires you to inform the manager of absence; benign but on a leash. I am being unreasonable but this is how it feels. Even if care has a light touch and is presented with the best intentions, it forces one to confront crumbling flesh and mortality. I am, at least partially, in the hands of others and have to fit in with their requirements.

Charged up, my mind slips back to the cult TV series *The Prisoner*. A retired spy is kidnapped and wakens to find himself in an idyllic but, as it turns out, sinister village, surrounded by mountains and overlooking a beach. Set in the village of Portmeirion (a fantasy creation by the architect Clough Williams-Ellis), all the inhabitants are known by numbers, so it is unclear who is on whose side – which are interrogators and which potential allies. When the protagonist tries to escape he is pursued across the sands by what resembles a giant plasmic puffball which wraps him in its embrace and returns him to the village[3]. I look over my shoulder as I take leave of absence. My son, Tom, says that if necessary he will come and help me dig an escape tunnel.

Very mixed feelings. Some have remarked that it is brave to assume the mantel of old age voluntarily, but it seems more like funk to me. A woman says kindly, 'you will be safe there'. My immediate reaction is rebellion, I don't want to be safe – and yet there is a small part of me that acknowledges the need for a pre-emptive bolt-hole in which to sit out the interim between an active life and death.

---

3   The Prisoner (1967–1968). ITV.

To relate these negative shadows to my current situation is absurd but affective states are notoriously labile. It is not only the loss of the nobody-knows-where-I-am-freedom that prompts such an association, but the fact that, in order to jog fading memories, when we flat residents introduce ourselves, there is a tendency to re-enforce our identities (and identification by names) with our room numbers. I am beginning to think of myself as Number 23 – resident in a circumscribed idyll.

Neighbours down the passage take a very different point of view. Increasing frailty led them mistakenly to opt for an old people's home which was, of necessity, dedicated to catering for the incapable. Everything was done for them, the only activity left in their lives was to present themselves for meals. For them, escape to this block of flats with support, sheltered living represents emancipation, freedom.

In making a record of affective responses, I am not necessarily proud of my reactions, or trying to justify my feelings at the time. They represent an ongoing struggle to come to terms with the inevitability of demise. I should like to avoid self-pity but given the subject, down-times creep in. For some, sadness comes in the shape of loneliness, people simply popping out of their doors to see who is passing by. Beyond this is the sharp edge of dementia; wraiths drifting in the passages, having lost a sense of purpose. A broken conversation erupts darkly into suspicion and whispers, 'I've absolutely no idea what is going on'.

In her poem, *Part*, Paula Jenkins uses a collage of the words spoken by a woman friend with dementia to capture the bewilderment and struggle of a human being (potentially you and me), trapped in a web of encroaching confusion. The thing called life happens in the third person, other people make decisions.

Part

We see it, we think it,
but we're not in it altogether.

One thing's taken off,
then another thing's taken off.

Everybody's lost their part.

In this place it goes on itself,
it moves so far, then not any further;

That's the mean part of it
and you hear the dogs talking about it.

They come here with red colours
and left alone colours
and absolutely bright whites
I don't know whose house this is.[4]

Unable any longer to speak his mind, a friend describes the boredom of Alzheimer's. Wherever it lodges, dementia is like ivy, its twisted shoots strangle the cortex: the sadness and pity and emptiness of it.

As a consequence, for those of us who are (so far) untouched by the scourge of entangled proteins underpinning dementia, labelling oneself as old by moving into sheltered accommodation is a life-changing decision – even if one makes it oneself rather than having had to be shifted involuntarily by Social Services when mice are found nesting in our beds, or we take to wandering the streets in a nightdress.

In an effort to make light of this decision, I enlist the help of two stuffed duck-billed platypuses who live

---

4   Jennings P (2015) *Under a Spell Place*. Glenrothes: Happenstance. Reproduced with permission. Happenstance.

on top of the radiator in my sitting room, emailing a friend: 'Archie and Mehitabel are moving house'. Such an indirect approach may sound coy but is easier for me to compose than the bald admission that I am not really managing on my own and am frail enough to need help. Big step downward, not unlike the nearby Stryd, a deceptive end-game – poised on the banks of the River Wharfe, where the course is narrowed abruptly by limestone boulders. Slippery edges wrapped in wet moss steepen the nearer one approaches the chasm, until all purchase is lost and the aspiring lover leaps short. Swept into subterranean caverns hollowed out by the compressed torrent. It is alleged that a body takes three days to resurface downstream.

However it's not necessarily death or concern about afterlife that is my problem. I gave up the notion of Hell some time ago – there are times when the idea of deep and dreamless sleep seems a pretty attractive alternative to life; since if I am not conscious I shall have nothing to worry about. As a friend says, dread is a function of being alive. Far worse are the indignities and loss of freedoms that accompany slow dissolution. And yes, the ever present burden one imposes on the (however willing) family, since medical advances now insure that we are outliving our generational span, overrunning the biological time when we can expect to be independent and useful contributors to society.

It is this no-man's land between life and death that is worrying since, unfortunately, the technical expertise of the medical profession has outstripped its capacity for compassion to the point where its goal is to keep the body of the patient alive no matter how many tubes it is attached to[5]. A typical medical student emerges with a focus on the heroic battle against disease

5   Gawande A (2014) *Being Mortal: Medicine and what matters in the end*. Canada: Doubleday Canada.

and only 20 hours training in palliative care.

'We've been wrong about what our job is in medicine. We think it is to ensure health and survival. But really it is larger than that. It is to enable well-being.'[6]

But while we are on the subject of longevity and termination, there is something to be said for standing back and understanding that, guiding hand or not, our lives and deaths are part of an unwinding process – and while each of us has a unique contribution to make, the world is not us: we are the proverbial grain of sand, an infinitesimal part of a whole. Having a sense of our place in the scheme of things gives us perspective. Mmm, all right for the rest of you but this is *me* we're talking about. Liverpool Care Pathways and cosmic detachment make fickle companions[7].

Scientists are not much better than doctors when it comes to understanding what is important during the process of dying. Those who seek to prolong life, as opposed to merely defeating its wrinkles, have recently been excited by investigations into the life cycle of a plankton known as Turritopsis Dohrnii[8]. A jellyfish about 4½ mm wide, Turritopsis is capable of regenerating when it gets old or encounters adverse conditions. Its tentacles shrink, its body withers, it sinks to the sea floor and turns back into a polyp, which buds off medusae that are genetically identical to the parent. In the laboratory it has been observed to reproduce this way a number of times, giving rise to the idea that its asexual perpetuation represents some kind of immortality.

6   Moody O (2015) Lack of training blamed as doctors fail dying patients. *The Times* **4 September**.

7   The Liverpool Care Pathway involves the withdrawal of food and water from dying patients. It was strongly criticised as being an excuse for palliative neglect and has now been discredited.

8   AMNH (2015) *The Immortal Jellyfish* [online]. The American Museum of Natural History. Available at: http://www.amnh. org/explore/news-blogs/on-exhibit-posts/the-immortal-jellyfish (accessed April 2016).

At this point, reincarnation comes to mind, an idea I've never really cared for since experience would suggest that once is enough. And in the case of the self-perpetuating polyp, not carried through in a style that strikes me as immediately attractive – imagine the practical problems. Worse still, it is likely that over a number of generations the genotype will deteriorate: imagine life as a failing jellyfish...

On the other hand, perhaps we *should* make an effort to hang on, since Japanese scientists have found that ageing cells in our bodies can be rejuvenated by dosing ourselves with extra glycine. Shrivelled mitochondria that are gradually becoming less and less efficient at the process of taking in oxygen and releasing carbon dioxide (thereby stacking up energy), can be rebooted. It works for rats[9].

And maybe it is this energy poverty that accounts for the tendency to drop off to sleep at embarrassingly frequent intervals, especially when visiting the lavatory at night. But the question such research does not address is whether or not we want to keep on crawling round a world that is rapidly falling apart and shows little sign of being able to repair itself? Even if we were to feel younger and are not just pumping botox?

Voluntary training on the use of a handy defibrillator reveals that a number of us in my sheltered accommodation have signed up for 'DNR', do not resuscitate. But in spite of carrying a warning medallion, it isn't clear how we can prevent the well meaning application of electric shocks, since the last thing would-be rescuers are going to be doing is rummaging through our bags or files to find the necessary red bordered certificate without which they are determined to continue.

9   Hashizume O *et al* (2015) Epigenetic regulation of the nuclear-coded GCAT and SHMT2 genes confers human age-associated mitochondrial respiration defects. *Scientific Reports* **5** Art. 10434.

We are living longer. In 1916, *The Times* thought it remarkable enough to record the deaths of four men and six women over 80. In 2014 there were over half a million people living in Britain aged 90 or over.

Too long. Although I resent the aches and pains of my later years, I have been extremely lucky in some ways, worked my ticket, and soon it will be time to go.

Malthus' prediction of overpopulation was correct. There are too many of us, or at least too many of us who have outgrown working age – and in this respect my generation's timing is poor. Whereas in Victorian times, Granny would have been tied firmly into a rocking chair in front of the hearth, nowadays families are dispersed: the need to address the problem of an increasing population of single elderly people who require support coincides with the government's desire for economic cut-backs. A report published by the Institute for Public Policy Research in 2014[10], describes the lack of structure to provide for a hidden population of elderly people with no-one to physically care for them or psychologically support them. In 2010, *Good Homes in which to grow old?*[11], summarised the arguments: at a time of financial stringency, there are more people growing old than there is housing provision available to meet their needs – and old people like to be consulted about the nature of such provision. And as a larger number of us grow old, the balance of elderly to carers (and workers contributing to the GDP) is tilting in the wrong direction.

Craven Council have grasped the nettle. In order to accommodate its increasingly elderly population (everybody's mother with the odd father thrown in),

10 Rose A & Davies B (2014) *Not Home: The lives of hidden homeless households in unsupported temporary accommodation in England* [online]. Institute for Public Policy Research. Available at: http://www.ippr.org/files/publications/pdf/not-home_Dec2014.pdf?noredirect=1 (accessed May 2016).

11 Local Government Group (2010) *Good Homes in Which to Grow Old?* London: LGG.

the local authority in partnership with a housing association has built my block of flats on the edge of town. To encourage a mix of communities, the town library has been re-sited from the centre of town to within the new block, together with a cafe and hairdresser, all with the idea of bringing the old and not-so-old together rather than segregating them. We do however lack a pub, and, excluding carpet bowls, an area that encourages exercise.

Nevertheless the flats are pleasant – and as one becomes available it seems it might be less painful to abseil down the precipice of age rather than wait for deteriorating circumstance to push one over the edge, even if the magnolia and grey decor is more encouraging of decrepitude than to an energetic lifestyle, and the cafe was having an off day when I visited. To be fair, it has since been taken over. It does function as a social hub, and makes great, calorific cakes.

There are conditions to meet. I must have lived so many years in the district and have family living nearby. There has to be physical need or evidence of mental deterioration. Apparently I satisfy interviews with the manager and a social worker, although I'm puzzled by the clause in my contract which, while it does not mention criminality, stipulates I must do nothing that is immoral. Where does this come from – and what in these days constitutes immorality?

I mention this doubt to the new Court Manager: perhaps it is all right provided I do not wish to start running a brothel? He warns me that it would only need two or three residents to follow suit and he could be liable for running a house of ill repute.

Not that I was contemplating a new career as a Madam but there do appear to be constraints. It's not just a flat I have purchased – shared ownership involves agreeing to be part of a system with boundaries.

The move involves registration at a different health centre. My new doctor asks me if I'm enjoying my flat: I have to stop and reflect how to answer since I am preoccupied with a different subject, that of admitting I am old, and publicly labelling myself so by moving into sheltered housing. Somehow I have to make it mine but at the same time dovetail myself into a community that already exists. With a bit of luck I shall be warm this winter since heating is part of the deal.

My first job is to paint over the magnolia, hiding its oppressive neutrality under cooking apple green, a restful colour but with a slight and intriguing acidity. And since the lights will always need to be switched on in a kitchen with no windows, I choose a warm night blue. The hall is white. It looks terrific.

Now that I've made up my mind, Margaret, my daughter, and her partner Kenny fill their van and simply move me while I'm away, lock, a somewhat diminished stock, and wine bottles, into two rooms, lining these with bookshelves, duplicating the downstairs room where I have been living to the extent that I am able to put out my hand and locate everything I need. My windows overlook a car park, so we hide it behind half-way curtains. Above the netting, a street of ancient cottage rooftops straggles up the lower slopes of Warrendale Knotts, a wonderful view when standing and when seated, filling the eye and mind. Facing east-south-east, the sun sets on their pie-crust flanks, picking out the walls and limestone epaulettes that decorate steep-sided shoulders.

I do have too much stuff. Before physically moving there is the problem of trying to condense a library, museum and art gallery into two small rooms. Sent by a friend to tease me, a quotation by Gabriel Zaid aptly sums up the situation:

'The truly cultured are capable of owning thousands of unread books without losing their composure or their desire for more.'

A bookseller takes two car-loads. Seventy-five full rubble sacks go to the recycling dump. I cannot keep all the paintings, there is simply not enough wall space, so some go to auction and the more special are given away. Among the latter, a couple of Rembrandt late etchings are passed on to a sculptor friend who is especially fascinated by his portrayal of eyes: each one gazes into and through the observer. She thanks me, sending the harsh but perceptive poem by Elizabeth Jennings about the artist's treatment of old faces.

Rembrandt's late self-portraits

You are confronted with yourself. Each year
The pouches fill, the skin is uglier.
You give it all unflinchingly. You stare
Into yourself, beyond. Your brush's care
Runs with self-knowledge. Here
Is a humility at one with craft.
There is no arrogance. Pride is apart
From this self-scrutiny. You make light drift
The way you want. Your face is bruised and hurt
But there is still love left.
Love of the art and others. To the last
Experiment went on. You stared beyond
Your age, the times. You also plucked the past
And tempered it. Self-portraits understand,
And old age can divest,
With truthful changes, us of fear of death.
Look, a new anguish. There, the bloated nose,
The sadness and the joy. To paint's to breathe,
And all the darknesses are dared. You chose
What each must reckon with.[12]

---

12 Elizabeth Jennings: *The Collected Poems* (2012) Mason E (Ed). Manchester: Carcanet Press Ltd. Reprinted with permission.

Rembrandt (and Jennings) are dead. But this courageous cross-fertilisation of artist and poet is a beacon, illuminating the murky traverse through old age.

How close can I bear to eyeball the actuality of my eighties, examining not only the noughts and crosses sag of ageing flesh but of sharpness of mind? It's not that I've been dependent on how I look. Just as well, since my flesh is beginning to resemble the worked-out wasteland I remember when we lived in Somerset: surface-mined soil, turned over and left in exhausted heaps, known locally as gruffy land. It hangs loose on my arms. Not at all comforting when scrutinised in the bathroom mirror.

Short sight helps avoid seeing too clearly a silky hair sprouting from the double chin.

But what of my old house, the friend I am abandoning? It's a shell now, in the hands of Catherine, plasterer and painter, filling in the no-man's land jagged craters left by repeated failed attempts to hammer picture hooks into limestone – and renewing coloured walls with neutral 'camellia', so that those who view the property (as I now have to think of it), can superimpose their own lives on it.

The papers are being prepared and my house and I are in the process of divorce – but as yet there are no suitors. In a village that has many empty houses waiting for sale, there have been numerous hits online but no-one has turned up to look round. I suspect this is because it had been mis-advertised as a barn (as it is) but one which has attracted prospective buyers looking for a rural retreat in the middle of a field, instead of a smallish semi-detached shippon next to the sheep market. Wrong clientele. Adding insult to injury, the agent describes it as 'quirky'. Enough to make any serious buyer back off.

Although we are separating, I need to treat my house memories with respect. It has welcomed friends and people I love and been the refuge and stronghold to which I have returned after long trips away teaching. It has embraced without complaint the books and pictures and antique mugs and jugs I've collected while I've been away. I have sat at my desk and corresponded with families and carers and therapists in Australia, South America, Germany, Canada and even St. Helena. Here, I've taught students from as far away Copenhagen and Moscow, written numerous poems and published nine books. It has been launch pad for intercontinental flights of imagination.

If I have to choose one memory, though, it is this. I am standing by the front door. It's early morning and a mist has spread up from the River Wenning. The edge is well defined and I'm in a pool of sunlight alongside the wall of vapour. A rolling cloud of stars silently folds in on itself – each pinhead mote sparkles – a Milky Way tucking in at my feet. I put my hand into the cloud and it comes out scintillating.

My brain is on the prowl, circling round and round the ability (or inability) to accept the markers of old age with their concomitant potential disconnection from mainstream living. As we get old we become used to slow decline, but as a friend who recently had a life-changing operation and is now totally immobilised says, it is the sudden lurches into irreversibility that are so shocking. We are so used to the medical model of being able to 'fix things' and now there are aspects of our life that bring us up against the concrete wall of mortality.

This far and no further. Already it feels as though I should be putting aside a penny bribe for Charon to ferry me over the Styx. Knowing the fragilities of elderly memories, the nearside bank of that last river must be packed with ghosts who, as Lucian suggests, 'have failed to equip themselves with currency that is legal tender in the underworld'[13] – or (perhaps more likely), we are frantically digging in the folds of our shrouds, since we can't remember where we hid our obols[14].

However, it's not only the experience of loss of personal capacity – 'I can't do this any more' – but also yours (and my) ageist images – 'she's on her way out', joining the 'moaning old women'[15]. In this random collection of the old, some on morphine patches or in severe pain, I've yet to meet with those who are not carrying on with the courage, dignity and the gruff resilience of their generation, 'We don't have a choice, just have to get on with it'.

These days, when it is against the law to use such discriminatory adjectives about race and gender, ageism seems to have slipped through the net, particularly with the unquestioned assumption that our elderly brains have deteriorated to such an extent that legitimate complaint is the product of imagination rather than a report of fact.

It's not just such overt discrimination – it can be more a more subtle ignoring of white hair. Last week, when struggling with an erratic sound system for a lecture, the technician discussed this over my head with the young speech therapist who had invited me to speak. Until at last I had to say, 'I think it's me you should be talking to'.

However, those who are not old (when does it start?) can't win, since the aged are sometimes deeply grateful for assistance (tender knees do not make a good launch pad to rise from a fall) and at others, irritated by it, especially if help comes in the form of tugging at equally painful arms and shoulders.

---

13 Lucian *On Funerals*.

14 A coin placed in the mouth of the dead as fare paid to Charon to ferry the corpse across the River Styx.

15 Sunday Times *Style* 17.05.15

Policemen may be getting younger these days but burglars are ageing. It was not only gold and jewels that led the pensioner's gang to rob the Hatton Garden safe deposit vault recently. Career criminals, they gave way to the temptation to try once again, one more spectacular to show the world they could still get away with it – 'if we get nicked, we can hold up our heads'.

But for those of us who are old, time has moved on without us, and eventually it was age that defeated these criminals. Their lookout succumbed to the handicap of shrivelled mitochondria and drifted off sleep. As a detective put it, they were analogue criminals in a digital era, underestimating the sophistication of contemporary surveillance. Having completed their heist successfully, this deceptively benign looking crew sat in a pub beneath a CCTV camera, bragging about their success and discussing how to divide the spoils.

Nevertheless, even if one of them was clutching a three-day supply of insulin in case he got trapped in the vault and used his bus pass to arrive at the scene of the crime, did these seventy-plus-year-olds really abseil down two floors of an internal lift shaft themselves? This schoolboy image passes into geriatric legend.

There to here

The move has happened so suddenly that in some ways I've hardly noticed the transition. In other ways, my mind is reeling. I need space to settle before I can write, to catch up with myself. Perhaps events will start to gel when I'm on holiday with a friend in her croft by the shores of Loch Eriboll. Or maybe, on return, I shall find the whole business was a passing fantasy: skipped dimensions, a 'what if' reality that never really happened.

Since roads are few the directions are simple: straight up the West Coast as far as you can go and then turn right. My ceramicist friend's house looks out over the loch to Ben Hope, currently draped in heavyweight cloud. A gale has been blowing since I arrived. The house is barrel shaped and anchored by thick cables driven deep into the rock. Plucked by each gust of wind, the cables bray with the deep rutting call of a donkey in love.

A week before I first met Lotte I had a dream. I was walking along a path beneath a towering cliff by the sea; the strata were made of books laid horizontally. At the time, her studio was part of a craft colony in a disused air force bombing range control headquarters. Her artefacts were like something I had never seen before – strange powerful shapes with colours from peat pools and lochens, encrusted with granite debris. In particular, there were ceramic books, with all sorts of marine sponges and stones falling out of their half-opened pages.

Lotte was surprised when the stranger suggested she had stolen her dream. I now have a number of her works, including one that is unique. My last but one visit, a stone deflected from her strimmer and shattered my car window. She swept up the fragments carefully. A month later, I received a parcel, a flat rectangular dish, her long deep sea-loch and the mountains either side, glazed with the reinforced glass of my car window. I keep my three pairs of glasses on it and laugh to myself every morning when I am trying to find out which is the right pair.

We have spent a comfortable few days talking through the storms. Tomorrow I shall start the journey south. I return to the question in my mind: where is home? Topographically there is no problem. I shall drive down to Inverness, through the grim Pass of Drumochter and past the fairy tale castle of Blair Atholl, where my great, great, great and-so-on grandfather reached out for water one night and mistakenly drank an agonising glass full of spirits of ammonia (Hartshorn) put beside his bed to wipe his brow after a stroke. In order to assuage the pain he drowned himself in the river. His body was recovered the next day eight miles downstream.

And keep on roughly in the same direction. Physically I know where I'm going. My family have done a great job of transplanting my goods and chattels. The psychological difficulty is one of 'hefting', a term applied locally to sheep. Turned out on unfenced land, a hefted sheep knows exactly where the boundaries of its pasture lie, where it is good to shelter in a storm and where the best forage is to be found. It does not stray. Although I can pinpoint my destination, I am not yet familiar with its ambience.

This sense of joining a community for the aged is reinforced when I meet my neighbour for second time and apologise for forgetting her name. She laughs and says, 'don't worry, we are all in the same boat here!'

Time slip backwards. In Oxford at the Ashmolean Museum looking at Anna Maria Pacheco's 'Ship of Fools', a disparate group of people in a boat without means of steering. Some are wrapped in shrouds, some are quite young but do not seem to understand their predicament. The implication is of crossing the river Styx, or being carried away in a process we do not fully grasp.

It is obscene to complain when at this minute the Mediterranean and the Andaman Seas are full of desperate refugees in sinking boats looking for any country that will receive them. I am ashamed, but even knowing this, I still don't want to be part of this terminal 'we'. I'm in the wrong boat, let me off!

Two points of view: on the one hand we have Dylan Thomas, 'do not go gentle into that good night. ... Rage, rage'[16] and so on – and on the other, the image of abscission: a spent leaf having done its job withering in order to give place to the next season's crop. Conscience suggests gracefully letting go – but hang on, this is *me* we're talking about! Never mind everyone else. Push, shove, I do not wish to be labelled as 'one of them'.

What are we to do about the old? Suddenly I am part of the problem, not agile any more, something askew in a balance system I've taken for granted ever since I was a toddler, climbed some steps and wobbled along the top of a wall, only to be told to come down at once or I would fall. But my eyes had lifted, opened; at 18 months I was entranced by being able to see a world over and beyond the head of my nanny in her cloche hat.

And then last year, I have a haemorrhage in my left eye and wake up one morning half-blind, the innate confidence of childhood vanished. The initial effect is of an unexpectedly lovely deep, deep, absinthe blue screen, with what appear to be a few small desmids floating around calmly. In spite of my distress I am impressed by their serenity.

---

16   Thomas D (1951) *Do not go gentle into that good night*. New Directions Publishing Corps.

In a day or so, beauty is replaced by a less entrancing reticulum, small fragments of a rusting network, patches of which I still see occasionally when looking at a white background. Mostly it is small grey areas.

Testing, testing. I spend months walking around with my good eye shut, trying to measure sight loss by such strategies as, 'can I define the feathery thallus of red seaweed draping a white pebble in the photograph on the wall, or is it just a blur today?' Since then there's been a tendency to trip over low-lying tables and lurch towards inevitable impact. Nowadays I keep my eyes down as I walk.

Occasionally a leg disappears, no message to the brain, simply is not there. Before I lever myself into the driving seat of my car, I outwit the potential treachery of this limb by a warm-up routine, making sure brain and foot are talking to each other, otherwise I may find myself prone on the tarmac rather than sitting at the wheel. Occasionally a fall is just carelessness when I'm not thinking about what I'm doing.

Time to rationalise. An ageing brain is preoccupied, scrabbling to keep up with the digital age, so who consciously thinks about their movements when they have spent a lifetime just allowing them happen? Learning to monitor contact, or lack of contact, with my place in space requires redirected and dedicated attention. Meanwhile I am fortunate to have a thick skull, am well padded – and the possessor of bones that may ache but do not fracture easily.

And how lucky compared with my mother's generation. Her hearing aid was heavyweight and cumbersome (when she did wear it – it was uncomfortable and almost unmanageable) and had a habit of sounding off penetrating ring tones at unexpected intervals. She was also nearly blind, as I should be had I not had the cataract operations that are virtually routine nowadays. She said she thought deafness was more isolating than sight loss.

Visiting an elderly relative, I remember being invited to speak to her through the mouth of a metal ear-trumpet. As a child I was apprehensive, it was so large I felt I might be swallowed in its maw. My aids tuck in neatly behind my ear lobes, invisible under a lock of silver hair. The first day I wore them, I walked out of the audiology department and was shocked to hear birds singing. But they do have one disadvantage in that they are apt to interact if I am wearing a lapel mike: the resulting noise can sound like workmen hammering on the roof.

At present I'm still allowed to drive since, having had a cataract operation, I can read a number plate at the required distance (although I am unable to specify exactly what this is, since the distance is expressed in metres, a measurement that that does not automatically paint itself on my road ahead). Overall, I'm pretty lucky in the physical sense, even if on the verge of needing help turning a mattress, more difficult now than it used to be – not only because of ageing fragility but because 'Dreams' have increased the thickness, weight and the consequent unwieldiness of their product.

But today mattresses are much more comfortable. Not at all like the thin pallets we slept on when I was at school, trying to mould our bodies round unforgiving peaks. At the beginning of term, we would scramble off the bus, rush upstairs to the dormitory and bounce on each bed to see which was the least uncomfortable. After a quick check underneath to see if any of the diamond steel mesh that supported the mattress in place was hanging loose (one cannot call them springs), we would bag our choice with a suitcase. In spite of the continual emphasis that was placed by school on our place in – and duties to – society, this bed-bagging ritual amounted to practical training in 'every woman for herself', me versus the ideal of community. Straight back to the most fundamental problem of all – how does the individual survive in relation to the group and what care should be devoted to its weaker members? (The alternative never occurred to me, that I should find the best bed and offer it to the slowest child.) So how do we develop and enact a social conscience against the biological imperative of self-interest?

I am trying to write an article about autism, picking my way with difficulty through a complex argument. A van is revving up below my window. The driver gets out, disappears, comes back, uses his iPhone, disappears again. This goes on for about 20 minutes. No hope of continuing to work. The only reason I restrain from shouting across the yard to ask him to turn off the engine is that it cannot go on for ever, he must come back soon. Surely he does not need to run it all this time? By now I have lost the thread and am completely wrapped up in hating him. And then the reception doors open and the most fragile and gentle of all our residents makes his slow, painful way across to the van door, steps with difficulty onto a lift and is hoisted up into the van. My personal inconvenience melts in consideration of the patience with which he bears the level of his disability.

This dilemma between me and 'not me' sharpens as I am inexorably shuffled from the role of care provider to recipient. The question, 'what are we to do about the old?' has become personal, 'what are you going to do about me?'

An unexpected feature of moving into a block of flats from a detached house is an increase, rather than decrease, in loneliness. Living on one's own, other people are not at the forefront of attention, but here there are constant reminders of their presence, footsteps, doors closing, voices, laughter. A persistent voice, like an accordion with a puncture, echoes round the yard.

Desperate to communicate, it hovers near the gate or hangs over the balcony, waylaying passers-by. I'll get used to it, like living beside a railway track and not hearing the trains, maybe learn to embrace its undulcet tones: but at present I'm over-sensitive, waiting for it to start again, squeezing constricted air through the distance.

If people are so important, it seems pretty shallow to be disturbed by a person who is blind and deaf and desperately trying to keep in touch with the world around him. The rules have changed – I feel like Alice in my new surroundings, as everything tangible falls on her like a deck of loose cards. Do I really like other people?

I want to be on my own; I crave solitude and space to write, but what are all these people doing out there? Especially what are they doing that excludes me? And what is that tapping noise? My left brain interpreter (LBI)[17] is working overtime on new stories to satisfy its endless quest for coherence, trying to make sense of what is happening. It needs careful training to steer away from paranoia – are they laughing at me?

In an attempt to throw some light on this capacity (or inability) to relate to others, I want to return to the subject of pronouns – 'I', 'we', 'you', 'they' – and, in a progressive stand-off from self, the contemporary usage of 'man', as an impersonal pronoun by London teenagers. An example is, 'I don't care how my girl-friend looks... it's her personality man's looking at'[18]. An even more extreme example derives from attempts to avoid causing offence: in the University of New Hampshire's bias-free language guide it is suggested that 'when introducing yourself to fellow-students, you should advise them as to which pronoun to you

17 Michael Gazzaniga – the circuits in our left brain are hard at work, trying to make sense of what is happening to us and turn it into a coherent story of our lives.

18 Cheshire J (2015) Mans cannot live on grammar alone. Innit blud? *The Times* **30 June**.

prefer them to use when they are referring to you in the third person: 'he', 'she' or the non-binary pronoun, 'zie'. Political correctness nose-dives into the death of meaning – oblivion.[19]

One of the minor irritations in life is how absolutely spot-on clichés are: it's difficult, especially for the writer, to navigate a passage round such pin-point accuracy. The one I have in mind at present is, 'absence makes the heart grow fonder', a Victorian sounding sentiment complete with a dreary beribboned Valentine card.

Separation from the people we love is painful, but nevertheless may expand our affective capacity – intimacy flowers from energy that might have been expended in physical relationship. Although modern technology can be an aide, in other ways it simply emphasises distance. The looking glass does not melt on Skype, I cannot climb through. Sometimes I want to smash its implacable face into splinters with my fist, as if by doing so I could be closer. This is end-wall, good for climbing the boundaries of information and even for sharing a new view – but hopeless for a hug.

We are forced to explore new ways, new sensitivities to other than ourselves. In some ways we resemble the jellyfish, testing the sentient waters of the undermind with myriad feelers, embracing the flow, responding to both positive and negative perception. So how else can I be with you who are not me but part of me?

Two 'I's add up to 'we' – but with a range of meaning from, 'We live in the same street' (accidental) to 'We have the same sense of humour' (still separate entities but now personally linked by shared affect). But in order to come closer, I need to explore 'thou', a word that has swung the full range from intimacy to disrespect.

Apart from its spiritual connotations, 'thou' is

---

19 Pavia W (2015) Anger grows at politically correct language that stifles free speech. *The Times* **19 September**.

archaic and has fallen into disuse. Nevertheless as Buber points out[20], although thou is too intimate to be spoken, it can be perceived as an expression of closeness, just no separation but communion. Our separate identities are lost in each other; I and thou are perceived internally as 'we' – a we that belongs in the language of lovers, a place where the most intimate flowering of self is fertilised by a profound awareness of other. Here there are no boundaries, just being in shared Being.

The unspoken quality of thou requires that we honour this other person as they are and do not try to bend them to our needs. If we are to arrive at this state we have to empty our minds, suspend our own blueprints and become a sensitive presence for other than self.

Without detracting from its quality, 'thou' has much in common both with the dyadic relationship between mother and infant and perhaps also with the experience of Winnicott's transitional space, where we exist for other, offering ourselves and discovering the contours of our internal landscapes through the mutual affective responses of our body language[21]. We are shaped by each other, growing through the joys we have shared – and hollowed out by the misunderstandings and miscalculations we have explored. We are mold and template, plastic to each other's needs, colouring each of our lives through this process of empathetic assimilation, becoming part of each other.

Contrary to the impression given by some self-help books, internalisation and integration require self-discipline and hard work. The affective 'we' that emerges is quite different from a free-floating

20   Buber M (1923) *Ich and Du*. Berlin: Shoken Verlag.
21   Ticho E (1974) Donald Winnicot, Martin Buber and the theory of interpersonal relationship. *Psychiatry* **37** (3).

vicarious enjoyment of second-hand emotion stolen without mutual engagement. (There is nothing more uncomfortable than a closeness that is assumed rather than shared.)

Yet once we have tasted the intimacy of such a relationship, what a student called 'the flavour', it remains built into the psyche. And we can revisit our bonded other at any time, and never really lose them. In this sense, my 'I' has become 'we' (you and I). We have become part of each other so that even if you die, your affective template is still present in me, even if it exists as the contours of pain.

The idea of emptying one's mind may be more familiar to those who practice meditation. But it is interesting to consider the work of Jill Bolte Taylor[22], a neuroanatomist who had a massive stroke that shut down the left half of her brain leaving her with the global impressions of cosmic unity characteristic of the right hemisphere. 'I could no longer identify the boundaries of my body. I felt enormous and expansive, at one with all the energy that was and it was beautiful.'

Maybe what we are doing in meditation is learning to shut down the left hemisphere of the brain, whose neural circuits specialise in creating coherent stories out of whatever is happening and provide the persistent background chatter that is such a feature of our mental lives. The trouble is that the left brain is heavily biased in favour of putting self in a positive light, a process that imposes my version of events on yours, making it difficult to experience the you that stands by itself, independent of my interpretations.

Letting go of self is not easy since we are biologically locked into self-preservation. As if it were a mantra,

---

22 Bolte Taylor J (2009) *My Stroke of Insight: A brain scientist's personal journey*. Hodder Paperbacks.

I hear my elderly mother mutter through gritted teeth, 'you have to learn to let go'. It is only now that I am beginning to realise what she meant; that is, not so much letting go of being alive – but as our physical capacities deteriorate, releasing what it is that has meaning in the sense of the stories we have constructed to support the image of our selves.

But before we can 'let go' we also have to learn to 'face up to' – they are part and parcel of the same process. The poet, Dorothy Nimmo, who is astringent and as hard on herself as on others, takes this message to its extreme in an excerpt from her poem, 'The Ballad of James Nayler', an unbending early Quaker martyr.

The Ballad of James Nayler

Most people know about fear
but most are afraid, They look
the other way, think about
other things because after all
they have to live.

But the warrior stays with fear
until he is all fear,
until the whole of his mind
heart soul strength
is in the fear
and then he will change
then he will go through
and come to clarity.

Some people know about clarity
but most are afraid. The light
gets in their eyes, they dazzle,
they would rather not see so much
because after all
they have to live.

But the warrior stays with clarity
until he is fully clear
and the whole of his mind
heart soul strength
the whole of his life
is in the light.

Then he will change
then he will go through
and come to courage.

Not many know about courage.
It is not something they need to know.
They watch a few set out
not knowing where they are going
and think they are going too far.
Most would rather not.
They have to live.

But the warrior stays with courage
until courage is all of his mind
heart soul strength
the whole of his life
which he will give up
and go through
and come to the cross. [23]

For those who might shy away from the spiritual implications of this ballad, here is a secular interpretation.

Life is tough – we all experience bad times as well as good. In order to shield ourselves we adopt a number of defensive strategies such as projecting our own scenarios on to others and taking in and colouring

23 Nimmo D (1993) *A Testimony to the Grace of God as shown in the Life of James Naylor 1618-1660*. York: Sessions Book Trust. Printed with permission.

our lives with their experience (introjection). If we are to grow up we need to withdraw our projections and lay down that which we have borrowed from others which is not truly ours. We have to integrate the themes we find difficult to bear and learn to look at, accept and carry our own burdens. It requires courage to look at and be mindful of the dark places in ourselves. But only when we are stripped of our own distortions can we look the world in the eye and say, 'I am here' – and more importantly, 'I am here for you'.

'Facing up to' allows us to participate in the process of living and ageing, rather than simply being ferried along as a passenger. It gives us room to be present for others, to listen, think about what others are saying and empathise, to be mindful of those who contribute to our lives[24]. We have to learn to give ourselves away in order to grow. Without the ability to listen we cannot really relate to other than ourselves.

When we are not dominated by our left brain interpreter it's as if we unexpectedly recognise a dimension that was hitherto unnoticed. Moving from black and white to colour, from flat to 3D, small details become important, we add to each others lives. In a different way, our lives become richer.

This roundabout digression allows me to get a clearer picture of what this community is or is not, at least in my own mind. Without a common goal to focus on, it is likely to remain a group of people brought together by circumstances rather than a group with a shared aim that might persuade us to suspend our individual trajectories. In these sheltered flats, our reasons for being here are largely negative, we are seeking 'refuge from', rather than embracing an ideal. Insofar as we

---

24 Krznaric R (2015) *Can you teach people to have empathy?* [online]. Available at: www.bbc.co.uk/news/magazine-33287727 (accessed May 2016).

are willing to join together, it will be with like-minded others. For example, a gardening group is emerging, united in our distaste for the shiny leaved identishrubs in neat rows, the mini plastic bushes that urge you to rub their leaves in disbelief that they could be real. We want variety, vegetables, fruit, a garden, not represented by the contractor's industrial planting scheme. Is there a possibility that we can have an allotment? A young man with a delightful grin says, 'I want colour, a patch of pansies, lots of colour'. It won't look so tidy but why not?

Meanwhile tranquillity is periodically invaded by a crackling intercom, which in theory allows us to call for help at any time – but for those of us who are even a little deaf is a font of indecipherable gurgles. This morning it erupted in strangled noises: three attempts later it emerged that clothing was now on sale in atrium until 1.30pm. Helpful pamphlets plop through the letterbox: the electricity suppliers have kindly sent a guide to assist the aged to know when their rooms are the correct temperature on a scale of 'too hot', 'just right', 'cool' and 'too cold' ('put on another jersey'). There are two problems. Firstly, the cunningly designed paper thermometer does not appear to respond to temperature fluctuations and secondly, while most of us are still sufficiently 'with it' to be aware when we are getting cold, if readings should achieve accuracy, they will be invisible to any of us who lack 20/20 vision. Glad to know someone cares.

Life of Reilly

The Protestant work ethic rolls its drums in the background. What is going on is a struggle between beating a dignified retreat and a rout.

I ask myself, what do the old do all day? Apart from spending much of their time searching for their glasses? Perhaps most frightening of all is the idea of a future filled with blank-diary days, when one will be unable to answer the kindly question, 'What are you going to do today?', since today is simply a nothingness to be filled between yesterday and tomorrow – without intention, without purpose, an abyss filled with guilt when the imperative to be useful has no remedy. Crocheting does not really fill the gap.

But the brain does seek stimulus no matter how circumscribed. A boy who is registered blind stands endlessly watching the flickering television screen. One of my ludicrous preoccupations is a game called 'spot the mouse', since this elusive cursor has a habit of playing hide and seek in the odd sightless crannies in my fovea.

But most of all one dreads losing connection with people.

The choice offered is stark. Keep active in mind and body, or lie back in an easy chair in front of the daily dose of low-budget reality TV. But in practice, muscular weakness and failing eyesight and hearing set limits both to physical and mental capacity. There may come a time when I shall look forward to watching celebrity me-time, yet another couple seeking refuge in the country or fleeing back to the cities, or following one of the endless programmes about food. After all, if I can neither hear the storyline or see clearly what is happening, it will not matter much if the content is pap. But not yet, please not yet.

This particular gloom is fostered by the week following Christmas; a week when the world out there is devoted to family pleasure and (irrespective of what is actually on offer) experienced by many of the old as one from which they feel excluded. It is the time when the number of Christmas cards are halved since many of our friends and contemporaries are dead. Irrespective of whether or not we are, it can feel as though we're jetsam stranded on a dried-out tide line.

Such sense of loss is not necessarily alleviated by laid-on entertainment. An old friend who is a nun, now physically incapacitated, has spent her life looking after the sick. She writes to me, tongue in cheek, that she now sees her role as being the subject, or rather object, of 'Corporal Works of Mercy', including parties and visits of tuneless choirs. (One of the more irritating features of the Catholic Church is its penchant for categorisation – every conceivable behaviour bears a label.) The switch from 'individual preference' to 'common denominator choice' is one of the hazards of being old. Good intentions are not enough.

I have yet to forgive the intrusive head of a hospital visitor that popped round the curtain drawn round my dying husband's bed and squawked, 'Being a good boy, then?' Peter was too ill to laugh: even now, my anger is a knot tied into the corner of my psyche. She was lucky to escape personal injury.

Sometimes it does feel as if one is being treated like a two and a half year old – and there are times when one behaves like one. Arriving back from Glasgow tired, I step out of my car, struggle with my bags to the side entrance, open the door with a fob key and dump them in the passage. Returning to the boot for more luggage, the door swings shut behind me. No bunch of keys – I've dropped it with my pack, which is already inside. Now I can no longer get into my car to pick up the last bag, or back into the flats to retrieve the keys and am instantly reduced to helpless rage. As if by magic, one of the staff emerges from the office waving a key. Back to the entrance, pick up key ring, back to the car, thank you for your smile and straightening out absent mindedness and incipient tears. Just for today there is something to be said for benevolent supervision.

However, at present, my peripatetic mind is both a problem and pleasure – one aided and abetted by Roget and Wikipedia, netting a new word, image or idea here and there – fostering a tendency to wander down intriguing alley ways. Does anyone else want to come too? Can I find my way back?

Outside number 23 – and after I've greeted his dog – a visitor from Toxteth tells me that we are living the life of Reilly in here, a phrase with which I'm familiar but not sure where it comes from. Enquiry suggests that not very much is known about who Reilly was or where he came from, except that he was an Irishman living the high life and an inspiration for a number of nineteenth century American music hall songs:

'He's money for to pay
so they let him have his way,
the best in the house is none too good for Reilly.'

Unlike Reilly, quality of life in these sheltered flats is independent of spending power. We are a socially mixed bunch, based on need rather than wealth, some residents are subsidised in one way or another. In practice, privilege is measured in terms of which bits

of one's life support system are online and which have
yet to be connected. A bit of a lottery. Whether or not
(we are constantly reminded) the inevitable faults in a
new-build have been addressed or ignored seems to be
dependent on chance.

Six months in and the red-hot underfloor heating
has been turned down in the flats, although not in the
passages and due to a mismatch of parts, not all the
toilets flush and some of us still have tepid showers. A
middleman precedes the plumber, a representative with
his company logo embroidered on his pocket, empowered
to see if I really do have a need – and no, he does not have
the correct key to reset the limiter on my shower, mine
is of an unusual design. And before a plumber actually
carries out any work, please will I sign this disclaimer in
case I should scald myself? How long will it take to get
this special triangular key? A week, a month, six months?
The rep does not know. By way of compensation he draws
my attention to an incipient heatwave forecast for this
week, so perhaps a cool shower will be an advantage?

Pressure is building. A visit from representatives
of the Housing Association is met by residents out in
force. Demands that action should be taken are skilfully
parried by the delegate who informs us that it is all
a matter of 'Health and Safety'. There is a system for
dealing with complaints known as 'Proper Procedure'.
Written requests should be submitted to the office who
will pass them to the court manager, who will deal with
them or pass them on. This way it will appear that any
failure is his, since if defects have not been remedied it
will look as if the paperwork is still sitting on his desk,
rather than being the outcome of a wrangle between the
Housing Association, the builders, the subcontractors
and the financial department as to who will pay for the
repairs. The manager is a sitting target, his desk drawers
alleged to be stuffed with ignored pleas and threats.

Frustration and anger bounce off the walls, to the extent that I begin to wonder if at least some of it stems from our new found helplessness – we have come from a world where we could arrange services and call in repair men who arrived and dealt with faults. Now we find ourselves in a situation of dependency. There is a growing demand for a legally empowered Resident's Association.

Three o'clock, Monday afternoon: a meeting of the steering group for a Resident's Association is moving from tentative agenda to action. Although all fifty flats were informed, five women and three men turn up, more than was anticipated since we have to fetch extra chairs, and enough to get started. A gathering of the aged (however motivated and intelligent) is not necessarily at the height of its sensory capacities. Although we have an obviously brisk and efficient chairwoman, a secretary and treasurer, deafness and an inability to recall names – even if we hear them – means that responses range from, 'Sorry, I didn't quite catch that', to silence that sits with folded arms and watches the world go by – and unravels the rest of us. We struggle to hear what is being proposed, leading to lengthy asides and breakdowns in coherence: 'What did you say?' 'What did he say?' A bit over the top: a few notes from a choral setting of *Paradise Lost* take over my brain. 'Confusion worse confounded'. Handel perhaps? Off we go again – where was it I sung that? Bit much for school, must have been a student. Back row of the Bach Choir, eyes on the conductor, mouth wide open, belting out, 'assails the prophet's ear'. He taps his baton, we respond as one throat to, 'Louder, I can hardly hear you'. We sing as one person.

But not necessarily as a committee. Call to order.

There have been some positive developments. Since the group first met, 'The Party with its Floor Show' has raised enough money to buy a barbecue set. Spar has been persuaded to donate three shopping trolleys

to the Court, so that shoppers can unload direct
from their cars and wheel their goods along the long
corridors to their flats. (The non-slip carpet drags on
the wheels and presumably also on those of wheelchairs
and mobile zimmer frames. It also catches on my
cleated soles, leading to a flying crash with the wall).
It is agreed that until a resolution had been formally
passed, the Steering Committee will work towards a
legally constituted association. All residents will receive
an invitation to a meeting to discuss this tomorrow
afternoon. Will I serve on the committee?

I am in two minds and at first I decline, partly on
the grounds of work pressure but partly out of concern
as to whether this is what residents really want. One
man expresses my doubts clearly when he says that he
and his wife wish to continue to live the life they have
lived previously and do not want to be pressured to
'join in' activities.

Since we are such a disparate group, the flow of
reminders to bingo, tombola, quiz nights and 'partying' etc.
which drop through the letter box with alarming frequency
are bound to meet with some resistance. A rather oddly
worded invitation to a 'death cafe', to chat about inevitable
demise, comes over as patronising to widows and widowers
and those whose mail is punctuated by invitations to the
funerals of their friends. The rot starts with bereavement
– we are familiar with death and no amount of counselling
is going to take 'never' away.

But there is a more subtle problem stemming from
our collective inability to see the world as others see it.
So maybe what some of us experience as patronising is
helpful to others?

Rumours and stories get around: each of us have our
own point of view. For some, the way ahead may be crystal
clear, while others are looking for an escape route, either
from an inability to make sense of what is happening,

Driving South to Inverness
© Pavilion Publishing and Media Ltd and its licensors 2016.

or from the terrors of their past. Protagonists see each situation differently: we are a skein of wool in the claws of a kitten – pull the wrong end and the rest snarls. And because we are dealing with matters of affect rather than fact, the more we try to unravel what happened, the worse the tangle. For someone who perceives an intervention as trying to direct them out of their 'comfort zone', even well-intentioned assistance may be seen by its recipient as intolerable pressure. In this respect, a closed community is like a pressure cooker lacking an emotional valve.

Perhaps it is misleading to think of us as a community – at present we are little more than a disparate collection of individuals gathered together in one place for negative reasons. Many of us would rather not be here, or rather, even if the flats are probably as good a solution to our predicament as is likely to be on offer, we are unhappy with the circumstances that brought us here. If there is a vague idea that we should act as a community I suspect it stems from an outside source which, for the best of reasons, envisages a fruitful and happy old age for its senior citizens.

So I want to follow what happens – and also to compare our situation with a truly closed community, that of a nearby Monastery of Bernadine Cistercians who I have got to know over the past few years.

Away from the village and set back from the road, the most obvious difference is that the nuns live according to the Rule of Benedictine – and all subscribe to a common focus, God. Secondly, they have all chosen to be there. And 'place' is important, although the Prioress says that the French word 'lieu' captures the flavour better: it's more than just a building.

A younger member of the community suggests that for her the meaning of this word may be a characteristic of Bernardines, since unlike other Orders where the Abbeys are autonomous, all the individual houses come under central direction so that the idea of place extends beyond the individual building and has to do with belonging to the wider community. Their vow of stability is towards the Order.

However, the community is made up of people who may be exceptional in their vocation but bring with them the foibles and weaknesses of the human condition. 'We may not have chosen each other but we do share a common belief which we try to live by, even if we are not always successful'. Since they do not often leave the building, there is little or no opportunity to get away from each other. So how do they cope with the inevitable stresses and pressures that arise?

Within the Rule there is a very comprehensive strategy for dealing with conflict and it needs to be seen within the setting of belief. At least once each week the community gathers in Chapter and after an appropriate introduction (a reading, either an excerpt from the Rule or from their constitution), there is an opportunity for individuals to say sorry, in a non-accusatory setting. The offering is received in silence and not referred to again, either inside or outside the meeting. In this way, a fault is acknowledged, apology is accepted and hurt removed. Very occasionally the Prioress may intervene if appropriate in specific incidents. In very rare cases, it is necessary to bring in outside help – but on the whole this system works well.

Wherever we are, we are people. We impinge on each other's space, get on each other's nerves. Even with the best will in the world, irritation, frustration, anger and hatred corrode our ability to relate. Nelson Mandela's Truth and Reconciliation Committee stands as an example of how learning to say sorry – and particularly the provision of an appropriate setting that allows this – contributed to healing the extreme wounds of apartheid. The process of forgiveness is liberating in that it breaks the chain link between perpetrator and victim.

What, if anything, can we learn from our very different situation, where we are living in a space that we are not yet part of? (In fact, less so than those of us who lived in a street before coming here, 'we were part of a community there, everyone knew everyone'). What does the process of reconciliation have to say to our random group of people gathered in a place with only a negative bond – that is, the fragilities bestowed by old age?

Alongside the easement of personal inter-relationships, present tension and stress is directed outwards towards external failures, notably in the plumbing system and failures in the accounting system. But already the paperwork generated by these has led to the departure of staff. And the whispered paranoia of dementia. At an individual level, learning to listen to each other and to say sorry when necessary is critical. But as well as personal oil on the water, to ease relationships there needs to be a structure to serve as the basis for action.

There's a weakness in the complaints procedure which fails to provide feedback as to when (if ever) deficits will be addressed. Having registered their complaints, residents are left completely in the dark as to whether or not anyone has taken note of the discomfort these failures are engendering. It would be nice to know that somewhere along the line a workman will appear and all will be well, particularly since the time-lag can be of the order of months and, it is rumoured, help may have to come from as far away as Cornwall. Trust gets lost somewhere along the line.

So, to return to the proposed Resident's Association, curiosity and a desire to know what is going on – and also a vague prodding of conscience about the necessity to be 'part of' rather than bystander – overcome my reluctance to join in. But first there is another problem, one that has to do with reputation, which I realise has preceded me when the night shift inform me that they have spent the small hours watching my work with autistic children on YouTube. Not really into status; an invitation to be Honorary President (presented as someone of some standing) sits awkwardly. However, doubtful that we shall be able to raise the necessary 60% vote in favour of the association – since aside from those who want no part in it there is a proportion who would find it difficult to make an informed decision – I accept.

A full meeting of residents turns out around 25 people, although some drift in late. Guided by the chairwoman we start briskly, approve the formation of a Resident's Association (independent of the Housing Association) to represent resident's concerns, and also the continuation of the acting temporary committee for a year. So no let out there. Following this, the meeting becomes bogged down in individual horror stories of varying relevance, notably circling around the shortage of parking spaces – partly because the car park is being used by dog walkers and general members of the public. Notices drawing attention to the privacy of the car park ordered two months ago are still on the production line. The meeting draws to a close with a determination that the committee will draw up a list of unaddressed problems and take them to the court manager. Meanwhile, a couple of turns with a small screwdriver resolves my tepid shower. Toilet still not flushing: one down and one to go. (And, in retrospect, more to come.)

Another visit, this time from a builder who pulls the flush, peers into pan, looks at me solemnly and assures me that it's not working correctly. I reply that this is a difficulty with which I am familiar and is the reason why he has been summoned. He goes away saying he will phone Doug. I write a note to the manager apologising for being so irritable.

Community, group, haphazard collection, or powder keg with the fuse already lit and spluttering merrily? At present attempts to organise the Resident's Association are falling apart and fuelled by anger. Coupled with the undoubtedly long list of real building faults, it comes back to a question of clashing personalities, seen as enthusiasm by a small group grabbing the bit between their teeth and galloping off over the horizon; by others as the ability or not to stand back and consider what is possible, or what is necessarily the best way of going about it. And when to resort to solicitors. On top of all this there are individuals who have their own problems and are stirring the pot. Unable to attend the last couple of meetings in my unlikely role of Hon. President, I'm brought up to date by a visit from two members of the committee. I am beginning to think that oil on the waters simply adds to the explosive mixture.

Some people have been here for six months and know each other. It's like being sent to a new school after everyone else has arrived. And because we are isolated in our flats, it's difficult to know who wants to be friendly – not everyone does. The least I can do is smile.

Still, back here and behind closed doors, we're all new kids on the block.

Organised by a resident, a Jacob's Join offers an opportunity to flesh out people from faces in the passage, listen to their stories. Being mostly in our eighties, whether or not we share interests, the one thing we do have in common and gets people talking is our wartime experience, not as participants in fighting – we were too young for that – but as children. Our memories of being evacuated, listening to the scream of a diving Stuka, bombs exploding and nights in the shelter or under the stairs are vivid. At first it seems exciting, bundled out of bed and sharing the mysterious night time with grown-ups, but mostly it is just uncomfortable, sitting on the floor with the skirting board digging into my spine – I can still feel the line on my back, exhausting. Wrapped in blankets, 'When can I go back to bed?' is met with a weary, 'Wait until the all-clear, dear.' Looking back it seems odd that these interruptions did not seem strange but, although we heard them, unless we actually experienced the shrapnel end of an explosion, children were protected by the calm and courage of adults. It was not callous – just happened in another street, not our direct experience.

However, one of the most vivid memories of my childhood is of being on a troop ship around 1941. Hearing loud bangs I ran on deck and asked a sailor who was leaning on the rail what the noise was. He said, 'we're fishing, look over the side'. White belly up, there must have been about half a dozen great fish, bobbing gently in the waves. It was not until later that I learned about U-boats and torpedoes. The depth charge must have stunned a pod of whales.

Returning to our party, here in our flats. There is a difference between getting to know about people and finding friends. I do find myself impatient for shared humour, the capacity to enjoy abstract conversation and empathy. How do we meet each other in this sense? Exhausted after a walk, I stagger into a pub and come across a couple from the flats. Perhaps the best way to get to know people is to trawl the bars at lunchtime rather than attend meetings.

A walk in the hills

In spite of evidence to the contrary, there are certain aspects of life such as dimensions that we take for granted. It turns out that I and the rest of us may be wrong, since mathematicians suggest that in order to explain the workings of the strange cosmos of which we are part, there needs to be not just the rather spooky fourth dimension, but many. So where are they?

In my student days we spent weekends in earnest debate as to the truth of the philosophical statement that there were trees in Hyde Park. Were they still growing there when oneself was not present? Nowadays we are more likely to be going on protest marches but the question remains, how can I believe what I cannot perceive? Does it exist only in my limited orbit?

More questions, this time about relativity and how astronauts age differently to those of us who are earthbound when the same interval has passed for both. And how does it come about that perception of an absolute is so dependent on the method of measurement?

This vaguely philosophical meander took shape a few nights ago when an extra second was added on to a minute, that is, at 11.59 we had a sixty-one second minute to permit the earth's rotation (which is slowing down), to catch up with our reckoning: a leap-second tinkering to which my brain, still clinging to the psalmist's notion that 'the earth is firm and not to be moved', finds it difficult to take on board. But the rotation of the earth turns out to be a less accurate standard for time than the oscillations of electrons in an atomic clock. Such synchronised finesse is critical for the world's stock market, which can trade and lose millions of euros, pounds, marks, dollars and yen in a second. Standing in the way of a permanent switch is a matter of national pride: Greenwich Meantime is British to the core. Out of sync with the sun, losing a second would result in the prime meridian, the temporal centre of the earth, drifting eastwards into France[25].

Of course it is not only the Earth that is slowing down, it's me too. My own perception of time is distinctly wobbly. Impatient when it lags, St Teresa resorted to direct action and shook the sand-glass to speed up her hour of prayer. And expecting consistency in so fundamental a property, why does time occasionally gallop over the horizon when we would prefer to draw out the present – and lie down and go to sleep when we are in a hurry?

Waking before five and switching off around eight o'clock in the evening, my biological clock has long been askew – these early hours, while the mind is still half-adrift in the undermind, are a good time for writing.

Looking out of the window, my horizon is shaped by the cloud level – and I suppose that the same can be said of how I feel in terms of affect. When mist drapes the tops like a wet flannel, the skyline closes in and I am hemmed in both physically and psychologically by a closer shoulder. The hills lean down and I should really much prefer to stay in bed. But today, at half past four, it's all clear, the sun is rising behind the beacon, dabbing red blushes on loose mackerel cloud. 'Red sky in the morning, etc...' But the shepherd is mistaken, the day turns out bright and beckoning. It's time to investigate the Warrendale Knotts. I take my car up the steep shoulder behind the

---

25 Whipple T (2015) Hang on a second, it's time to let the Earth catch up. *The Times* **30 June**.

nearby village of Langcliffe, negotiating its hairpin bends with care, looking for a good picnic place for the future. Near the top, several long distance footpaths converge overlooking the Ribble Valley, by now splashed with sunlight. Below my feet the land drops sharply to the silver river winding between trees, a quarry hides the massive remains of Hoffman's lime kiln, a 19th century monument to a vanished local industry. Further up the dale, the drumlins rise and fall like green bubble wrap, backed up by limestone crags and millstone grit tops.

Ordnance Survey maps started life as a military requirement to survey Scotland in response to the Jacobite Rebellion in 1745 – and widened to cover England during the Napoleonic wars. My map, OL2, stops just to the east of an ancient rifle (musket?) range on the opposite side of the valley. From my window I can see the cairn marked on the top of Knotts. I should like to stand beside it, an ambition rather than a practical option given the state of my knees, 'elderly wear and tear, nothing exceptional – one can expect it at your age'. As part of their village celebration, Lancliffe have organised a poetry competition. I think it will be a good idea to see what I can write.

My first version mentions Sampson's toe, an eight foot rock standing guard over the village. Legend has it that Sampson broke off his toe when he tried to leap from one side of the Ribble valley to the other. A more prosaic and likely explanation of this massive rock balanced on stilts, is of an erratic dumped by retreating glaciers. Perhaps it is over scrupulous, but not having actually been there and rubbed my hands on its surface, I decide to leave it out.

Langcliffe

*A huddle of grey cottages
clusters round the green,
turns its back on the road north:
penned between river and scar,
the village is easy to pass by.*

*A fault in time slips to shallow seas,
to sediments of microscopic shells,
sifts sand to grit, to the burden of ice,
to melt, moraine and an eiderdown
of drumlins upstream.*

*But for birds, the quarry is silent,
car park to a visitor attraction,
information boards describe
the repeating kiln, sweating men,
crushed limestone, sweated rock.*

*The furnaces are cold. Children play
hide and seek, a litter of Pipistrelle bats
squeaks and squirms in the flue,
iron-stained stalactites drip from arches,
Hawkbits climb crumbling walls.*

*An unshorn ewe trails shags of fleece,
pennants without breeze;
as I trudge up the Pennine Way
twins scramble for her teat,
refuge as much as milk.*

*Crossroad to footpaths
fanning out across the karst,
Langcliffe is a reliquary
for the half-remembered;
who would want to leave?*

Parking on close-cropped turf, I set off tentatively
up the Pennine Way. Although a track, the stone is
loose and slippery, rutted with rainwater run-offs and
I place my stick with care. The bridleway follows the
side of a wood steeply for some way and then bends
sharply left to follow the side of a wall towards Jubilee
Cave. At this point my legs tell me to turn round
and go back while they can still respond. So much
for adventure. Descent is slow, walking down is more
precipitous than going up.

The hillside is scattered with sheep and their
lambs, the unshorn ewes looking scraggy, half cast
fleeces dragging like damp rags. A lamb balancing on a
knoll nods its head so I nod back. We begin a delicious
conversation. Each time it shifts its head up or down
or sideways, I copy it. Instead of running away to its
mother and grabbing her teat (as would have been the
normal reaction to proximity of a person), the lamb
becomes attentive and still. It starts to watch me very
carefully and then to turn its head deliberately in one
direction or another and look back at me to see if I will
respond. Step by step it works its way closer to me.
Eventually its mother calls and it runs back to her.

When I get back, I highlight in yellow the distance
covered, a couple of inches lost in the folds of the map.
Pathetic – but in psychological terms an achievement,
mind-washing when there is a danger of settling back
in my room and sitting out decline. I meet my neighbour
and tell her where I've been. Without self-pity she says,
'I can't do that any more'. I ask her if she can get in a
car and we arrange that next time we'll go together – at
least we can have a picnic and look at the view.

But to go back to the lamb and our interaction using
body language. Today I am in Scotland at a school
for children with complex needs (blind, deaf, autistic,
cerebral palsy, the complete spectrum of developmental

dysfunctions), filming and taking stills for a book on autism and attachment. The school feels happy and quietly competent – it does not reflect the twisted limbs and circumscribed expectations of its students. My job is to introduce an approach based on using body language rather than speech to develop emotional engagement, particularly with children with autism, although it can be used with many children with whom we struggle to communicate.

A small girl is led into her classroom where the level of disability is such that the staff and support teachers spend most of their time changing the students. Her expression is what one might call 'switched off', there is no light or curiosity or engagement in her face. She seems in full retreat, in another world, but she fumbles her way to the computer and tries to turn it on – her teacher says this is all she really wants to do. That and sit on the sofa, which is used as a reward for having completed a task. So I suggest she comes and sits down. Although she is not obviously doing anything, she looks round out of the corners of her eyes at the room with four strangers in it, the camera men, the producer and myself, as well as her teacher and support worker. After a while she makes a very small sound, almost a mew, which I answer. Very tentatively she makes another and we gradually build up a 'taking-turns' conversation. I ask her teacher to sit beside her and press her back each time she makes a sound. (In addition to answering her sounds with sound we are using pressure to reflect the pattern and rhythm of each sound). She starts to smile and her sounds become more frequent and confident. Our response to her sounds has become a way for her to communicate. In a world that is totally confusing, they have meaning for her: she has become alert and interactive in a way that her teacher says is different.

For those on the autistic spectrum, the strain of trying to make sense of incoming speech (and other signals) using a faulty processing system causes acute anxiety. When we use their body language, we bypass verbal processing and tune into each other in a way that is less stressful than speech. Comments on such behavioural transformations range from, 'it's as if we are finally talking to them in a way that has meaning' and, 'I've never seen him want to be with people before', to mothers who say, 'I've got happy kids now'.

But I realise how fragile I am when my editor/producer sends preliminary stills: we see them from completely different points of view. In one I appear to have no teeth and in another, I'm requiring assistance to walk. She sees wisdom, I see falling apart. Something in me explodes. It feels like being tied to two wild horses which are being flogged apart.

If we don't die, people who get old and have a particular gift (with a massive label of urgency attached) are caught in a double bind. The principle emotion is utter rage directed at an increasing physical and mental inability to fulfil what is so urgently required of us. What irks especially is a romanticising of old age – wisdom, courage, awe, all that sort of stuff – when the necessary energy is running away like rats from a sinking ship. It leads people to fixate on personality rather than process – 'How can you do this when you are 80?' But age leads us down a blind alley, all this tells us is that we are failing to direct attention to the message we are trying to get over. I knew twenty years ago that this was going to happen and I hate getting out of sync with what is required, while at the same time recognising that there will never be an end to this. It's like trying to clean the Augean stables, endless shit, an impossible task: hence my sensitivity and tetchiness. I email my friend and editor – 'in this joint venture, let's focus on trying to demonstrate again the skill of giving intimate and bonding attention. There is nothing at all to celebrate about creeping dissolution.'

To calm down I walk up the leafy path into town and pause as usual in front of the bookshop. This time there is a display of second hand Penguins, including *The Big City*, subtitled 'The New Mayhew' by Alex Atkinson and illustrated by Ronald Searle. Wedged between aisles of thrillers I get comfy on a stool. The pages fall open at 'An Actress of Advancing Years'. I quote:

'Her upright, elegant posture was not quite natural. I received the impression that she was at some pains to maintain it during our conversation, as perhaps during a performance on the stage. There showed sometimes in the expression of her eyes a hint of apprehension which mocked the stubborn jauntiness of her remarks. From this I concluded that she had not (as I first thought) altogether persuaded *herself* that all was well.'[26]

She goes on to describe how she is now unemployed, 'there is nothing much doing at the minute', but clings to her work, wraps it round her like the cardigan she is wearing to maintain her identity and keep herself warm.

On the opposite page, Ronald Searle's portrait sits elegant and erect in the corner of a chair. Bony fingers play with her necklace. Her lined face is a mask that fails to conceal etched in anxiety and sadness. The sketch ends with a small drawing of her when she is on her own, slumped and looking out at a row of houses. Her face sags.

The bookseller remarks that Searle's accuracy is often cruel. Like Eleanor Rigby, who keeps her face in a jar by the door, both Searle and the Beatles pinpoint the necessity of maintaining a facade, keeping up appearances against the onslaught and isolation of old age. Forcibly torn from everything that contributes to

26 Atkinson A (1958) *The Big City: or The New Mayhem*. London: Perpetua Books.

our identity, we are flotsam, adrift from everything that makes us ourselves.

Mmm. I admit that my work is as an integral a part of my life as I am of it, one might want to call it fixation. It would certainly be easier to let go of one's past life if the need were not so great. The biblical observation that 'the poor are always with us' seems callous, at odds with the general message that we should love each other – but if one thing is certain it is that however much we try, demand will always outstrip supply. And yet each child is important, and they and their family's suffering can be alleviated if we learn how to communicate with each other in such a way as to reduce their anxiety. Even if it is as little as a grunt and smile. So I go on, sitting at my desk, answering the phone and emails, hammering away at programs, books, with excursions to see individual children and give talks to parents, professionals, teachers and therapists, trying to show as many people as possible that we can help them to communicate with their families. I suppose that this is how it will always be until I keel over. And I'm grateful for purpose. It is not just that I cling to the work to preserve the notion of who I am. I'm entranced by the revelation of each person I work with.

Pictures at an exhibition

A hot night, and sultry; thunder rolls round the hills. A fireball breaks loose from the jagged edge of fork lightning and streaks across the sky.

The move has caught up with me and I'm tired, really tired – not just physically but psychologically exhausted. Steamrollered. Tripping over box files, running out of paperweights, even the heavy pebbles looted from beach walks, my desk and tables are a blur of paid and unpaid invoices and bills. Paperwork is building up to the point at which it will soon have to be stacked in piles stretching away down the corridor outside my front door. I don't know which bits should be filed where. And it's no good filing them online, since unless I can see them they are deleted from my consciousness. If they are visible at least I can worry about the chaos.

Yesterday, I was overcome with a deep sadness to the point where I cried, a desiccated weep without tears, just an involuntary metallic wail grinding up from the gut. There did not seem to be an immediate cause but it felt as though I was sitting on rock in a dried-out stream, drowning in the grief of absence.

Like autism, too much data, and the brain crashes. We reach a limit and then shut down. But it's not only those on the spectrum: in an alarming recent experiment, fourteen pilots were flight-tested landing on a simulator. Signals that a cross wind needed to be allowed for – and another warning of an undercarriage failure, were fed in simultaneously. Disastrously, eight failed to pay attention to the emergency message[27].

When I was small, my mother, who was a violinist, would sing me to sleep with a lullaby, 'Matthew, Mark, Luke and John, bless the bed that I lie on'. My father, when he was there, would follow this up with, 'Twinkle, twinkle, little star...'. Pitch was not his strong point. But I felt anchored by their strength and drifted off quickly.

Nowadays, going to sleep is more of a problem, lying back wondering if it will happen is not good news. Why can't I just switch an off button? And more infuriating, why is it so impossible in retrospect to ensnare the feeling of going to sleep? Why do I wake not knowing what the act of going to sleep feels like? I miss the last crucial step every time.

No, there was once. I'm staying at the Abbey, reading the Epistle of St. John. Whatever you think of it, Jesus describes his relationship with God, 'He in me and I in him'. Being in Being, we can't get closer than this. I lie back in Presence. It's the only time in my life I am aware of the act of going to sleep – as if I am being swaddled, right over left, left over right. I watch the light in my mind being snuffed out and the next morning and today, I remember that instantaneous switch-off of consciousness.

Unable to recreate such certainty, I'll take a detour round my gallery (equivalent to counting sheep). I should explain that this haphazard collection of paintings, ceramics and et cetera have been gathered on nomadic journeys round the country, normally on the way to some engagement or other. Some have been given, others acquired after considerable economy and

---

27 Hookham M (2015) Pilots' brains 'crash' in crisis. *The Times* **5 July.**

consideration. Downsizing requires what our politicians, who lurch from one cliché to the next, pronounce as 'difficult decisions'. Each object left behind (or perhaps I should describe them as subjects since they each possessed personality), was done so with regret, each retained has an affective tag.

Instead of the four Evangelists, angels do feature in a small pair of pictures on the wall opposite my bed. Gilt framed secular icons, both are painted in red and gold. In the first, Icarus tumbles from the sky as the wax on his wings melts, shedding leaves (rather than flight plumes, since the artist had an unusual antipathy to feathers known as 'pteronophobia'). Below him a squad of awkward angels stretch out the corners of a Persian carpet to receive him. Only one is paying attention to his imminent arrival, the rest are looking at the viewer.

The companion to this painting is an Annunciation. Gabriel hovers with a propitiatory bunch of flowers. I smile every time I look at these two.

Dead now, James Martin, who painted them, also constructed automata. His paintings are extremely precise, almost tesselated, as though there could be no other possible interpretation of the image in question. Even a spiritual subject always appears slightly tongue in cheek – but painted with meticulous seriousness.

Nearest the door are three small china plaques. Two are antique, stern, unsentimental and unadorned invitations addressed to sinners: 'Behold God will not cast away a perfect man, neither will he help the evil doers' and, 'Sinners obey the Gospel-word, hasten to the supper of my Lord, be wise to know your gracious day, all things are ready, come away'. The last one I bought is suspect, probably a modern copy, bearing the straightforward admonition 'Prepare to meet thy God', a message old age feels it should take seriously, just in case. Nevertheless I envy such certainty.

Promenade: coming round to the wall by my bed, a Turkoman rug conceals a second and superfluous door to the bathroom – and separates a drawing by Joash Woodrow from a small secret photograph that is difficult to categorise. Two weathered pieces of wood (an impish round knobbly head peering out of a fork caused by a knot) are side-lit. Lorna Graves, who I can only describe as having given birth to this idea said – and I agree – that it was rare that a photograph was better than its original subject. On the back, she has written. '*Genius Loci*' – the spirit of the place – and has added '*for Phoebe*'. This one is personal. The frame has a tendency to creep sideways however I adjust the wire behind it, to the point where I feel that it is making a wabi-sabi statement and I should leave it askew. Its tilt is part of its impertinent charm.

To return to the Joash Woodrow drawing, or rather to the artist himself, the story of his life and arrival on the public scene is more than unusual, an art dealer's dream come true. Browsing in a second-hand bookshop, Andrew came across two ancient volumes whose pages had been extensively scribbled over. Inclined to put them down, there was something about the quality of the sketches that led him to investigate further. Joash, who was not difficult to trace, turned out to be a hermit, living on his own and who refused to let him in. Eventually, he grudgingly admitted Andrew. The house was stuffed with paintings, thousands of them; paintings of incredible power dashed onto any old canvas, sacking or handy material, using tarmac or any old media. The brushwork of his portraits, particularly of Hasidic men wearing their hats, is so direct: one stroke for an eyebrow widens, pivots and narrows without pause at exactly the right angle – so simple, extraordinary. His landscapes are usually of houses and gardens fenced in by white palings, obsessional in a way that, combined with his eremitic nature, suggest that Joash may have been on the autistic spectrum. Bought by universities and businesses, his paintings now command prices in the hundreds of thousands of pounds.

Joash is relentless, gives no quarter. His sketch on my wall is of an ageing but lively, rouged-up woman strumming a guitar, a whole world suggested in a few lines torn from a sketch-pad. Not sure my mother would have liked it.

At this point on my tour I am looking for a seat, one of those squashy buttoned leather benches provided in galleries to rest feet, backside and senses. But at the head of my bed is a print by Philippa Troutman, one of six of her works that I had before I moved but had to whittle down to four. *A Cock and Bull Story* is the original of an illustration for a book of poems by Ian Duhig inspired by the tale of Tristram Shandy. Again, it's difficult to describe a picture in words. That is, one can describe images and dispositions but miss the feel. This picture is a variety of cadmium reds, carmines, vermilion and pinks, rhododendron colours. Realised as an open book, the cockerel's head is on the left, the bull, with its suggestion of the hidden child we all contain, is on the right. But it is also about the line that escapes the discipline, an erratic and perhaps erotic energy, crowing in the erect comb and hence into the picture. This is the sleight of hand, where art breaks out of illustration and leaves me open-mouthed.

The pictures are deliberately grouped so as to try and avoid cluttering the walls. I drop my eyes a couple of feet to a modest landscape south of the Crinan Canal. A small lane trickles between the sea and a harvested forestry plantation. Apart from the stand of dead firs outlined against the horizon, usable logs have been removed: what is left is a spilled matchbox of small branches and brushwood. Having climbed over a couple of fences, I'm back sitting amongst gorse bushes, hot yellow flowers setting fire to the landscape. I'm wishing I were better able to reproduce the perception I have of space and dereliction. Why can't I put on paper, not so much what I see, but what it feels like?

Next to this is a small etching of the walls of Jerusalem by my father, who started out as an artist and went to the Slade but was swept into the trenches of the First World War.

Only three more works to go on this wall. *Moonlit Bay* is by a Scottish artist, L B, of whom I know nothing but was captivated by his/her(?) abstract juxtaposition of delphinium blues that suggest moonlight without lapsing into silver. And as with the cock that crew, there is the escape pod, an inexplicable scarlet trailer...

The second is a drawing by Alan Thornhill, bent double with vertebral disintegration, pushing his art materials around in a pram. A group of people with superficial faces grab each other with elephant trunk wrap-round arms, mouth synthetic party kisses: 'mmwah'.

Finally, a block-mounted procession of sheep crayoned on cardboard by my preschool son. Drifting from left to right, some are grazing, others have their heads twisted upwards in the air. Collectively they have that continuity of a flock, many individuals with a common focus – in this case, eating.

Ah, one more picture by the window on the far wall: another by Lorna Graves. Lorna spent most of her artistic life exploring her undermind, searching for her Animal, a female figure that appeared in dreams, much the shape of a polar bear with many pendant teats. One day she took me to a nearby churchyard where a king had ordered a well to be sunk. Passing travellers could dip the bronze cup into the crystal water and refresh themselves – and so it had remained through the centuries until someone stole the cup. It was replaced by a tin one. Lorna was deeply affected by this blatant rape of history and charity. Lowering the cup into the well became symbolic for access into the darkness that haunted her work. There are many sombre paintings and prints of cups or vases falling into the well that reflect her journeying.

The year that Lorna died she told me she was trying to find a new way of painting landscapes which moved beyond accurate representation to expressing the feeling of a place. She produced very few but they were extremely simple. One, which I gave to my daughter, was of a Cumbrian field in the snow against a tyre grey lowering sky. Only two colours, but a dealer who saw it spoke with a voice of awe, 'I think this is the most beautiful landscape I have ever seen'.

That last day I went to see her, I stopped at the bottom of the narrow stairs and looked up to the landing. Light from the window was streaming onto an oil painting tilted against the back of a chair to dry. I caught my breath. The unframed picture throbbed, pulsated: as if the still-wet canvas had trapped and was holding on to sunlight. Although I recognised the cup theme, this was completely different from her earlier and more sombre treatment of the subject that had haunted her for much of her life.

While we ate lunch she told me she had long wanted to paint poppies in a cornfield but not in the conventional style that decorates so many gift cards painted by Manet. And here it was, broken out of depression, a synthesis of the blood red poppy as cup, resting in a fierce tawny-gold landscape. Near the centre of the flower is a violet indigo smudge, cumulonimbus, the colour of thunderstorms, standing in for the cluster of anthers. She said it had taken two days to summon the courage to enter the dark smear. Without it, the picture would have been nothing but red on orange, interesting colours but lacking the power and definition that holds my attention.

A long walk round a small room. Taking a step back to my son's sheep, by now I have gone to sleep, which was the purpose of this perambulation, or I suspect so, since knowing sleep is largely retrospective and I shall not be certain until I wake in a couple of hours' time, this being the average tolerance of my bladder.

What next?

Margaret and Kenny come today, bringing flowers and herbs to grow on my balcony and roses from their tiny garden for my bedroom. Every time the window is open and wind blows, plastic fragments litter the floor so Margaret rehangs my curtains with metal hooks.

We sit over a cup of tea and look at the flat. The books are in place and the Archangel Gabriel stands serenely on the low cupboard between twin bookshelves. It's been fun anticipating, planning, measuring and executing ideas – six months nest-building, choosing the right piece of furniture to slot into position. Everything except the loo works. It's finished.

So what next? In a way, all this activity has been stalling the big problem which I return to now – what do the old do? How do they fill in time?

Yes, there is still an avalanche of professional work but whether or not and how I can continue has been thrown into doubt during a routine check-up at the Ophthalmology Department, which coincides with an age-related application for a new driving licence.

The consultant looks up from his computer and announces that my test results for lateral field vision are borderline for driving. This is a total shock, since my long sight is excellent and I've driven at least 23,000 miles without mishap since the eye haemorrhage eighteen months ago. The apparent deficit relates to a visual field test for peripheral vision, sitting with my chin cupped into position and one eye covered, looking fixedly at a bullseye and pressing the button, or apparently failing to do so, every time a random pinpoint light flashes on the target. But it seems artificial: I don't drive with eyes fixed dead ahead. Spending so much of my life driving a van has taught me to rely on side mirrors and my head is constantly scanning side to side to check up the entire scenario. One eye compensates for any deficit in the other.

Meanwhile I'm waiting for a buff envelope from the DVLA to thud through the letter-box, worse almost than one's final results. LBI (Left Brain Interpreter) is panicking, considering possible and impossible alternatives. It depends how desperate people are for training – locally, some will come and fetch me. I can teach two people a time here in the flat. Two old friends have offered to be drivers.

Living day by day, I can only wait. And in some way I feel oddly detached from this life changing possibility. Perhaps it won't happen. But what if it does?

I do the sensible thing and go out for a drive before the DVLA tell me not to, south to Preston and then back cross-country along designated quiet lanes, where the only vehicles I meet are a double decker bus, which (presumably having visited the Wild Boar Park nearby) pulls politely into a farm gate – and nearly home, a speeding coach which comes round a right angle bend on the wrong side and misses me by a couple of millimetres. Apart from these excitements, my afternoon is spent in an idyllic traverse of the Forest of Bowland, beside stumbling streams and along narrow tree-lined tracks striped with sun. The banks are carpeted with pink, red and white campion, buttercups and sheets of ox-eye daisies punctuated by groups of foxgloves – all except one slope which was clearly seeded from a commercial wild flower packet, bright and cheerful, but its alien flowers are out of place. Curious, they would have looked at home in a flower bed but its nodding marigolds are uncomfortable pretending to be local.

The sheep on these farms have been shorn. Relieved of their heavy fleeces, they are bounding around like wild goats. The electric clippers have left tramlines on flanks daubed with red paint.

I return by Stock's Reservoir and its encircling forest (last time, a hind with two calves crossed in front of the car), up the long hill to the rocky crest where I pause. The Forest of Bowland gives way to the valley of the River Wenning. Beyond, the Dales are splashed in sunshine. Pen-y-Ghent, Ingleborough and Whernside rise from their limestone plateau like yolks sitting on the whites of poached eggs. I may need to remember this.

Bits of memories are scattered all over our cortex, like books in a library with the hippocampus as index, in the sense that it knows where they are – and also as librarian, accessing and joining up the different fragments[28]. (I suspect my librarian is using an alphabetical filing system since I can so often remember the first letter of the name or file I am after but the rest of the word is blank.)

By observing an epilepsy patient undergoing brain surgery, researchers at Leicester University have actually been able to observe a new memory being initiated by a single cell in the hippocampus for the first time[29]. Half angry, I want to keep in mind every twist and turn of this journey (in case).

So remember this journey, make new cells so each rock and stone is imprinted for all my time.

28 Buzsaki G (2006) *Rhythms of the Brain*. New York: Oxford University Press.

29 Quiroga RQ (2015) *Celebrity Selfies Helped Us Uncover How Memories are Formed in the Brain* [online]. Available at: http://www2.le.ac.uk/offices/press/think-leicester/science-and-environment/2015/celebrity-selfies-helped-us-to-uncover-how-memories-are-formed-in-the-brain (accessed April 2016).

Reviewing the options, I feel guilty if not working, not only because there are so many people who need the help I can give, but also because the Protestant work ethic was drummed into me at an early age. When we visited him, my great uncle, Keeper of the British Museum, said to my mother, 'She's very pretty but when will she learn to think?' I can't have been more than about five and didn't know what he meant by thinking but it was obviously important.

Current occupations on offer for the elderly such as line dancing and craftwork feel like colouring books for children to keep them quiet on a car journey, or worse, a magic painting book that simply required me to dampen the page and colours would appear. Water flowed everywhere as did the merging inks. All the pictures faded into a soggy blue. Time fillers but no skill required.

The struggle to keep the mind going is balanced precariously against inertia and the temptation to retire to bed and read thrillers. Oh for the days when the aged were allowed to be bed-ridden!

Wait, wait and see... what happens if nothing happens?

There is writing and poetry – I am permitted to do these but both require subject matter, inspiration and energy. Walking is encouraged because it is exercise, but there is a nasty sharp pain in the ball of the right foot which throws my balance. Nevertheless, the weather forecast is fine for tomorrow so I shall rise early and take the car up to Malham Lane and see how far I can get.

There's always desire to find out what's round the next corner. Misjudge it and walk too far, up and over the rim: fields open out into a shallow bowl. Attermire Scar with its caves peels off to the right and the lane stretches away to the east, up and on over the next ridge. A waller is repairing a corner of the wall, his eyes fixed on the pile of stones at his feet, searching for a particular irregular shape. He doesn't need to try it on the wall – once he has spotted it, it slides perfectly into place. Although he is young, he already possesses the skill of perfect attention. Poised as a heron fishing, there is nothing else in his mind. It stirs a poem in me:

No Lucky Dip

The young man
stands by the wall,
scans the stack by his feet
for an irregular shape.
All his intention is in the search,
a heron seeking the strike:
his eye
knows what his brain is looking for.

When he spots the stone he's after,
the Waller darts down,
pulls it from the pile,
slides it in place, beds a perfect fit.
He has no need to turn it round.

Neither does he answer
when I pass and call. He is
already attentive to the next slab.

Returning home, the dreaded buff envelope lies on my doormat. More forms requiring all sorts of information I haven't got, such as the names of all the consultants I saw nearly two years ago – never the same one, it felt as though I was a component on a factory line being shuffled from one to another. 'Sit in the row of chairs on the left, not enough chairs, wait, test, sit there, wait, eye drops, wait, Mr X, Y or Z will see you now, more drops, wait'. In/out, no idea who it was: should have gone armed with a laptop and taken notes. But the upshot is the DVLA are giving me extra time while they try and sort out if I am fit to drive. The fall of the axe has been stayed for six weeks.

Bumping along the bottom, I return to the idea of being in a place but not part of it, not belonging. As one ages, this sense of displacement is temporal as well as spatial and relates to community in general as much as individual circumstance. Grandpa Simpson complains that he used to be 'with it', but then they changed what 'it' was. It's difficult to know not only where one is – but also what it is that one is aiming at. The goal posts have got dry rot, crumbled. Ropes and safety netting lie tangled on the ground, trip the unwary. One of the phrases from school that sticks in my mind and is probably echoed by each generation, is from Cicero's bitter attack on Catiline, 'O tempora o mores', which translates roughly as, 'Alas the times, and the manners'[30]. Or a phrase from *They Saw It Happen in Europe, 1450-1600*[31], 'the world goeth fast from bad to worse'. The reference points of language and culture we took for granted no longer embrace meaning. Behaviour has changed: we cannot assume basic observance of respect for others. Money and celebrity value have replaced class as social determinants. On a different scale is the introduction of the young to violence and hatred for political or so-called religious ends. And why has it become acceptable to show torture porn on music videos? Related to this is what Obama calls the 'empathy deficit': research suggests that in America this is accompanied by a fourfold increase in assaults on young women.

However, although processes are slowed by the weight of bureaucracy and an inadequacy of funding, the outlook

---

30 Cicero, 4th book, second oration against Verres (chapter 25) and First Oration against Catiline

31 Routh CRN (Ed) (1965) Blackwell Publishers.

is not all that bad, much has changed for the better. Even if they are slow to respond, we are protected by health services, social services – and there are many people working hard to alleviate suffering. An open society is an ideal, even if it has not yet shaken off corruption.

Last year I wrote a chapter titled 'Belonging' for a forthcoming book, trying to untangle how this sense of feeling secure in a familiar place had evolved in my life. Since it was wartime, my father in the RAF was frequently moved – and sufficiently senior in rank for his family to be moved with him. The consequence of this was a permanent uprooting, an absence of peer group and the family as the unit of focus. My mother unpacked and repacked 17 times during the five years of the war. It was a life punctuated by having to burrow in crinkly silver-foil lined tea-chests to locate a lost soft toy, or later on, a precious book. Smells and sounds are evocative and the dry tinkle of tea-flakes spilled in the bottom of the box is part of my childhood. Knowing my mother, I suspect we were drinking them the next day.

I keep coming back to the idea of how one manages transition from a solitary life to living within a community, however loose it is? And the subsidiary question about how I should relate to it?

Before we can develop this feeling of belonging we have to be able to differentiate ourselves from our background. We cannot know other if we do not experience ourselves as different from other; we have to be conscious of ourselves. As well as from my designation as No.23, I need to know who I am before I can know you or relate to you. That is, a labelled map of relevant features is not enough, in order to really listen to you, I have to have an affective awareness of myself, be in touch with myself emotionally. In this way I become a listener rather than defender of my own territory.

Chicken Licken

Chicken Licken

Last week I was teaching the residential staff at a boarding school for children with very severe physical disabilities. Rated 'Outstanding' by Ofsted, they also have some children with autism but the night staff have had no autism training at all. They look at me blankly and say, 'we don't know what to do'. And they don't, they know nothing at all.

It's a hard day's work and I'm tired by the end, tired as a drained hourglass lacking the energy to turn itself over and start again. On the way home I drive in by the back way, a small road that wriggles down from the town between Georgian cottages, through the car park and into the rear entrance. At the top of the slip road, a woman is standing and waving her arms, stabbing the sky with all the urgency of Chicken Licken trying to convey imminent Armageddon. I slow down and she bangs on the car. Her grey eyes are full of agitation, even terror. I try to wind down the passenger window but the child lock is on and it's jammed. I am as cut off from her as she clearly feels from me, too stupid to understand what she's trying to tell me. Exasperated, she throws up both hands, gives up and turns away. Her coat flaps in the wind. I don't recognise her and don't think she is one of ours.

Sitting down to write, I note the collective 'ours', and reflect that my centre of gravity has shifted – the 'we' I rejected is starting to take shape. The ambience is filling out, small things are becoming important, moving from monotone to colour.

The best walk starts opposite the entrance to the flats. Brockhole Lane (presumably the home of badgers, or Watery Lane as the locals call it) is narrow and walled on both sides. Possibly because it is not grazed by sheep, its verges are a riot of flowers.

My memory for flower names is almost as bad as that for people, a deficit when I read botany at university. Those I do recall are from a school competition when I was around ten. The idea was that we should gather wild flowers, bring in samples and have them ticked off a list. All went well at first since buttercups were readily to hand, the lawn was covered with daisies and the walls dripped with ivy-leaved toadflax. But as we roamed further afield a member of staff with an ecological conscience realised that 150 children were stripping the countryside of rarities. The final straw was Herb Paris (the True Lover's Knot), a strange looking plant with what seems to be a black pearl set in a rosette of leaves, normally found in Scottish woodlands, but unknown in pastoral Somerset. Our efforts were brought to an unexplained halt.

The lane is studded with deep blue geraniums, swathes of yellow stonecrop dangle over a stone trough built into the wall and the air is weighed down with the blousey smell of meadowsweet. After the allotments, the path narrows where it is joined by a shallow stream running beside the path. The sun highlights lacy patterns where water snags on pebbles. Further up on the left is the ruin of a magnificent hay-arch.

All idylls have downsides and mine is balance. Fallen twigs and sharp stones hide under swathes of grass ready to trip the unwary. Enticement lies round the next corner: over the wall, woodland concealing a bronze age settlement. As ankles and knees protest, how far can I get?

After around quarter of a mile, the lane ends abruptly in a T-junction with a large handy milestone,

just wide enough to sit on and contemplate the view
– sheep pasture, woods and walls. To my right is a
creaking barn, corrugated iron sheets flapping in the
wind. It makes me aware of how alone I am, an old
fear that has stalked my explorations ever since I
was a child evacuated at the beginning of the Second
World War to a Victorian mock castle on the Welsh
Borders. Full of dry rot, its crumbling towers belonged
to my cousin Gee who was in her 90s. She had been
a suffragette and, it was thought by the family, was
sufficiently intimidating to man the ramparts and repel
invaders. My cousin Elizabeth told me that the woods
were full of German parachutists dressed as nuns.

So what does one do with these irrational fears, the
shadows of self-preservation that flit from tree to tree and
lurk behind the wall? Keep walking, keep on walking.

Coming back down the valley, Pen-y-Ghent looms
over distant foothills. Butterbur leaves the size of small
umbrellas flap in the breeze. The undersides are pale
with stems like prickly rhubarb. My spirits are lifted by a
beautiful walk: collateral damage, ligaments in shreds and
blood blister on the middle finger squashed between two
stones when subsiding on a broken piece of wall to rest.

Today is another day and I need to go to the bank
and also to collect the wheelbarrow full of medicines
that keep me alive from the chemist. Instead of the
more usual Yorkshire scarecrows the town has chosen
to celebrate its summer walls with flowerpot sculptures.
A great deal of ingenuity has gone into the production
of dragons and spiders. A flowerpot pony leans over the
wall of the local vet. I am moved to give him a carrot from
my shopping basket. (The next day I am not entirely
surprised to find it has been munched, a hungry snail
has climbed up the escallonia and made a meal of it.)
Moving into town, a family occupies the seat outside
the post office – I feel inclined to move the baby onto its

mother's lap so that I can rest my feet but fear the infant might fall apart in a cascade of pots. Native Americans camp by the old police station. However, my favourite is the all-black Dalek outside the toy shop. Correct in every detail, it only lacks voice. I visualise it as the Town Crier, marching up and down past the Shambles in the square, 'Oyez, oyez, exterminate, exterminate!'. A colleague emails me to ask if I would be honorary president of the (excellent) service she has set up for engaging with disabled children and adults in London. I am honoured and send her a selfie of myself with the Dalek for publicity. She replied that they would be very happy if my friend would serve as Hon. Security Officer!

Twice in so many months it occurs to me that one truly knows one is getting old when invitations to be Honorary President of this and that start to roll in. 'You don't have to do anything but it would be lovely to have your name': active to decorative passive.

The local supermarket, Booths, seems to be a neutral ground suitable for casual encounters – and these reflect the full range of personality. First, I make for the newspapers and am accosted by a stranger who is scanning the stand. The pictures are of drowning refugees. His moustache bristles fiercely, as he turns on me and says, 'I tell my wife, we should send them all home, tell them our pavements are not lined with gold'. Telling rather than listening seems to be his preferred method of communication. He moves off when I suggest that we may be sending them home to pavements swimming in blood.

Having filled my trolley, progress in the check-out queue has ground to a halt while the supervisor disappears to find out the price or availability of some purchase. A woman tells me how much she loves living near the River Ribble. When she was a child she had never seen a river, except as an illustration in one of her books:

two children playing on grassy banks by a stream. She pestered her mother to take her to visit one. Eventually she was taken to see the Manchester Ship Canal. A great brown slug of unmoving water – big disappointment. I respond by telling her that my husband's firm had made the shovels that the Irish navvies used to dig the canal, paid at the rate of four and a half pence an hour. When Peter was a child, the canal was a superhighway, ships plying in both directions, a bone of contention, stealing trade from the Port of Liverpool and conveying it to the heart of Manchester. At the opening, his grandmother sailed in the barge behind Queen Victoria. Now it seems empty of purpose.

On the way home I call in at the tourist information office to collect a list of B&Bs. They haven't got a new one but I'm welcome to write down the phone numbers off their four year out-of-date one. So I sit down and copy them out onto an odd bit of paper fished from my pocket, only to find on completion that it is the back of a stamped letter on its way to the post box. So I recopy it and borrow a bit of paper and Sellotape to tidy up the envelope. As I hesitate to rise after sitting chatting for some time, the tourist officer describes my difficulties as 'rigor in the ramparts'.

Why all these stories? My nest is complete and attention shifting from anxiety to enjoying possibilities – but at the same time there is a risk that the diary will become just a string of anecdotes. Perhaps I should use them as pepper to be shaken over the page occasionally – and turn my attention to the book about autism which I should be finishing and with which, lacking the energy to re-engage, I've slightly lost touch.

Nevertheless there's just one more – well, one and a half...

Last week I was driving in the Yorkshire Moors with a friend and we rounded the corner in a village called Lastingham, which grew up round a medieval church noted for its extraordinarily beautiful Norman crypt. Looking like long-necked gargoyles silhouetted against the setting sun, two giraffes, complete with ears and horns, were peering over the parapet of the tower. Open mouthed, I nearly swerve off the bend. Imagine the insurance claim and explaining to the police, 'Yes Officer, I did come off the road and through the wall but there were these two giraffes standing on the tower'... 'Just breathe into this bag, Madam'...

Giraffes have a fascination that their shorter-necked cousins, the okapi, lack.

I once stopped by a B&B to ask for their phone number. The landlady who opened the door had her hair in colossal rollers. Behind her in the hall was a near life-sized papier-mâché giraffe with a see-through neck. Before I left I asked for an explanation. She explained it was for the village fete; the children could climb some steps and roll pennies into the open mouth for charity. She added that she had made it during the long Northumbrian winter – 'we need something to do in the dark evenings'. As a subject I don't think giraffes would have occurred to me, elephants perhaps, vases, bowls?

Or a handy biodegradable urn? Something you can put on the shelf while you wonder where to scatter its contents?

After Peter died, I spend a number of holidays beating out grief in the hills round Littondale. A heron stands immobile by the source of Cosh Beck. A rough track follows the stream up from Foxup to an ancient barn. Once inhabited and half buried in nettles, a window in the shape of a cross looks out of the ruined wall and down the dale. I thought perhaps it had been a monastic building but Unc. told me shyly, 'some hippies lived there and one of them had got religion'.

While still an infant stream, a bridge spans the beck. Too narrow for a drove road, its unmortared arch is grassed over and only one stone deep, perfect. The water stumbles over shallow limestone shelves for a couple of fields to join Foxup Beck, together they source the River Skirfair. Not far downstream it vanishes into a vast system of caves, largely unexplored since two young men drowned in its caverns and the farmer closed access to the entrance. Added dyes confirm that the river that continues down the dale to join the wharf is not the same as that which plunged into its depths upstream. It seems a pretty good destination for ashes. And rather less chancy than maritime disposal: sailing into the wind on a breezy day, mourners at a friend's burial at sea spent the return journey picking minute shards of bone out of their hair. Or consider the fate of my husband's colleague. Asked to accompany back home the remains of a scientist who had died while lecturing in Austria, he was woken at the Swiss border and asked to get off the train and bring the necessary papers to the station master's office for verification by customs. While struggling with bureaucracy, his train and the ashes silently departed, leaving him to travel back to London in his pyjamas.

Which brings me to an explanation of where I am now.

Induction

Not quite sure why, but as the owner of Flat 23, in order to complete my induction forms I'm required to share a potted version of my life history. The question is where to begin?

I am five years old, kneeling on a chair leaning across a polished Chippendale table where, in response to my questions about family, my mother has opened a long scroll and is explaining that this is her family tree. As far back as you can go – in fact a lot further, since it starts with Adam and Eve: a favourite kick-off point for Victorian genealogists. Apparently it is quite simple once you get on to the Old Testament and who begat who. There is a slightly hazy link between imaginative construction and the loins of the Black Prince (Edward of Woodstock) who was an early exponent of Blitzkrieg, pillaging and burning his way through France and fathering a number of illegitimate children. He died a few years before his father, so never actually succeeded to the throne. His epitaph is gloomy:

Such as thou art, sometime was I.
Such as I am, such shalt thou be.
I thought little on th'our of Death
So long as I enjoyed breath.
On earth I had great riches
Land, houses, great treasure, horses, money and gold.
But now a wretched captive am I,
Deep in the ground, lo here I lie.
My beauty great, is all quite gone,
My flesh is wasted to the bone.

Peter points out to me that at the time of the Black Death the population was so reduced that who one was related to was largely a matter of sticking a pin into whoever one fancied.

As the generations passed, lineage becomes rather better attested in the form of documents. There is a a Ducal portrait on the staircase in Blair Atholl. He is notable for having changed the face of Scotland by introducing forestry to its hills. The 13th daughter of the 13th duke (I think), married a parson in Shrewsbury. Her father built a mellow Queen Anne house in Shropshire, suitable for his daughter to live in. There followed a series of 'gentleman farmers/Indian Army', offspring of the latter being sent home to be brought up in England since the Indian climate was deemed too harsh.

Aged five, my mother was put on a boat home from India, without parents, to grow up in Great Ness with a bunch of cousins. The children were looked after ('overseen' is a better word) in a desultory way by seven great aunts and a succession of governesses, who left rapidly since their charges proved unmanageable. My mother, being the oldest, got spanked by all the aunts in turn for misdemeanours.

Six of the aunts lived in the main house, the seventh had been relegated to the lodge after having had an affair with the coachman. There was also Great Great Aunt Julie, who travelled round Afghanistan alone for two years, apart from a large retinue of porters carrying 30 odd trunks wrapped in white linen piped with red trimming. My mother remembered that there was much excitement when she finally returned, as it was supposed her boxes were full of jewels and would restore the waning family fortunes. As it turned out they were packed with toilet paper; possibly a scarce commodity in the mountain villages?

By now, living memory is supplemented by parish records and faded sepia photographs. My mother is standing with her two brothers and younger sister holding a pony. All are dressed in starched white, the girls balancing immense cartwheel Victorian hats. One day she heard a man playing the violin and decided that this was what she wanted to do more than anything in the world. So she was packed off to Germany aged 14 to learn – and ended up living alone in Czechoslovakia just before the First World War broke out.

Recalled, she found herself housed in Cheltenham with a straight-laced family from whom she rapidly escaped by marrying my father, Roderic.

Rather less is recorded about Roderic's family than my mother's, except they also served the Raj – but as tea planters and missionaries rather than soldiers – until his father (my grandfather), who was the first of the family's academics. MJM Hill was a fine mathematician. When they were boys, his sons, Roderic and Geoffrey, already budding engineers, designed and flew a glider off Hampstead Heath. The Hill Glider, as it was known, used to hang from the ceiling of the Science Museum. With updating, it has been moved to storage. Working at Shorts in Northern Ireland, Geoffrey, my uncle, went on to design the first delta wing aeroplane. Known as The Pterodactyl, it was so ahead of its time that no engines could be found suitable to power it. Instead, my uncle showed me a model in a small mahogany box. My Aunt Gwen, MJM's daughter, became professor of oncology at University College London.

MJM's intuitive talent has leapfrogged several generations to his great-great grandson, who says he just does not understand what the difficulties of maths are – he just sees it. For those of us in the intervening generations who shudder at the very thought of calculus, distribution of talent seems a little arbitrary.

My father left school to study at the Slade under the fearsome art teacher Henry Tonks, but joined the Northumberland Fusiliers in the First World War. When the Army selection board asked him if he thought he could become a leader of men, he replied that he did not know. Reluctantly they sent him for officer training, knowing that the life expectancy of an officer at the time was six weeks. Wounded and decorated, he returned to England and joined the fledgling Royal Flying Corps, becoming chief test pilot at Farnborough Experimental Station, flight testing many of the early fighter planes.

In the Second World War he was in charge of the air defence of Great Britain during the V1 attacks, taking a stripped plane up (to increase its speed) and flipping the flying bombs off course by inserting his wing below those of the missiles. After the war he went on to develop the technical side of the RAF. When he retired, he was appointed Rector of Imperial College and subsequently Vice Chancellor of London University. He died aged 51, found sitting on a park bench in the City. He was smiling.

Roderic, my father, Dad: a larger-than-life figure from whose creative embrace it was difficult to emerge. Unexpectedly, I saw him on TV last week, on a program about the Second World War, talking to King George VI, showing him round some installation. Here he is for a moment or two, handsome in his uniform, leaning forward in deep conversation, animated. Although this is a second-hand cameraman's snapshot rather than personal memory, the affective presence of him wells up inside me. I feel him. Even now he is my plinth.

Ancestors: farmers, soldiers, adventurers, heroes, intellectuals, the good, the bad and the occasional nasty tucked away in a corner cupboard – it feels a lot to live up to.

Meanwhile my recording angel is beginning to look at her watch and I wonder if she is going to get through to the present before her shift ends. So perhaps I should delete further exploration of the forebears (along with the ashes of the Chippendale furniture – and my soft pink rabbit with a red nose, burned to a crisp during the Blitz) and start with myself.

Having moved house so frequently, my memories are a straggly procession of pop-ups, snapped in different places. Roughly, they divide into pre-war, wartime and post-war, dominated by wartime. Strange things happened: in retrospect they seemed totally normal, it never occurred to me that life could be lived in other ways. The passive acceptance of a child is so well expressed by contemporary usage of 'whatever?' accompanied by a shrug of the shoulders. Still, odd things stand out – the convoy to America and being told that if I need to jump over the side of the ship I must tug my life jacket down or it will break my neck (although why I should want to jump overboard is not explained – it seems a long way down and wet when one got there). My sister Prudence and I collect sacks of acorns in the woods to feed pigs. I learn to draw Hitler's face with one line and a splodge for the moustache. And there are chilblains, white skin peeling off raw flesh like a layer of onion.

At home there is the ominous drone of the doodlebugs. My mother explains that when the noise stops it means the engine has cut out and I must hide under the bed. As a life preserver it looks second rate, not quite up to an Anderson shelter.

Two sweets a week supplemented by squirts of toothpaste dried on a radiator on the odd occasions when they are working, is precious bargaining currency, traded with cousin Tim for a fragment of doodlebug, very light weight, which sits now on the shelf over my desk. He threw a bit of shrapnel in as make-weight.

Both my brother, Peter, and sister, Prudence, are much older than I am. Prudence is away teaching, so I am virtually an only child. My brother is killed flying into a mountain when his engines cut out. The rear-gunner escapes and is looked after by Italian partisans. Found crying on the stairs at school, a teacher offers the following counselling, 'He was brave, so you must be brave too'. Succinct, to the point – there are so many of us who had lost brothers or fathers and occasionally mothers and sisters in air raids. It certainly turns off the tears.

On the home front, change from war to peace happens at a snail's pace, principally because the aftermath drags on in the form of rationing, near bankruptcy of the country and a general exhaustion.

Education is sketchy. Due to the high turnover of staff we study the three-field system seven times and then skip lightly to the Victorian era. In retrospect, by far the most interesting thing that happens at school is being taken down a working coal mine, the last of the North Somerset coal fields. A small field, the seams are high quality but contorted and of uneven thickness so that mechanical extraction is impossible; the coal is hand-won, hewed out lump by lump.

I am afraid of lifts but acceleration is so gradual that we do not know we're moving until one of the miners holds up his lamp. The walls zoom upwards at incredible speed. Deceleration is similarly unnoticeable. We walk underground single-file along a narrow gauge railway track towards the face, stopping beside a bell shaped mould in the wall, dreaded by miners since it easily slides downwards, causing rock falls. The miner stops and tells us to put out our lamps so that we can know darkness. It isn't so much frightening as totally different from previous experience, something we are totally unprepared for.

Night was never so dark. Extinction is positive, not just absence of light but it has substance. Blackness stuffs my eye sockets and nostrils and ears, its inky fingers wrap my throat. I am without perception of sight, smell or sound.

When their candles ran out, child workers in the mines used to sit in this darkness, regulating the hatchways.

Lagging behind, some of us get separated from the main party and make our way towards the sound of voices. Round the corner we come upon some miners hacking away at the face. Hieroglyphics of sweat trickle down their naked backs. They look up, surprised by the appearance of three grubby girls. Pointing to a narrow chute in the wall into which they throw the coal as they dig it out, one of them says, 'I can hear your lot in the road below, you'd better slide down that and join them'. Terrifying – but somehow I stuff myself in and using my hands as paddles squeezed tight against my chest, push my body against the slope, emerging onto a moving belt below like toothpaste coming out of a tube. Breech birth, I turn to watch my friend's legs dangling from the chute and being delivered into the arms of a relieved teacher who has only just realised some of her charges are missing. Born again; one suspects that health and safety regulations would have taken a dim view of this life changing expedition.

More postcards: I leave school with some relief and an exaggerated gesture, tossing my grey school hat into a bin at Paddington station before catching the tube home. The following year is spent filling in the gaps in my education, catching up at a crammers in Holland Park. We are an odd bunch. Jemma, an English child who has lived in Ceylon, spent her formative years in a local school squatting on the ground learning the Koran, then two years dancing with the Ballet Rambert. Ann has a passion for archery unmatched by skill. Since there is no range we practice in the street at night. I still recall walking up the steps into a Kensington hotel and asking the porter if I can have my arrow back. He returns it impassively, as if handing back lost arrows is part of his job description.

Success! University College London takes the top off my head and gives the brain a good stir, prizes open my eyes. Shell shock at the first lecture when Dr. Ross discusses something called the palato-pterygo-quadrate bar (the changing shape of which I seem to remember is crucial in the evolution of reptiles), drawing this bone on the board with his right hand and erasing it with his left as he crosses the platform. At the end, I crawl out, muttering to my neighbour, 'what the hell was that all about?' But gradually, from blackboard to laboratory to library, volume to dusty volume, microscope slide to slide, I start to learn what the business of thinking is, the fascination of following trails and closing in on the centre of a problem. Dovetailing the apparently irreconcilable, sliding errant facts into a pattern, is a pleasure almost akin to orgasm.

And I meet Peter. Introduced by a friend, he asks if he may join us for coffee. I look up into the most astonishing eyes, sea-green with a pale circle round the edge, like that slither of light trapped under the crest of a breaking wave. And a gentle smile that reaches from one side of his face to the other. Never having been truly in love before, he might as well have been wearing a T-shirt emblazoned with the words, 'This is the man with whom you are going to spend the rest of your life'. Just like that for both of us. His colleague protested, 'You can't marry her, she's the Vice Chancellor's daughter', to which he replied, 'I can and I will'.

He is also a fine pianist and takes to practising in the evening in the lecture theatre at the bottom of the steep flight of stairs up to my department. Lured by crashing chords, I creep in to listen. Incredibly shy, for the next two years we eat supper together, somehow continuing to pretend each evening that we have met by accident.

Resistant to practice at first, it now turns out that two of our offspring have inherited Peter's musical talent. Thomas, who started off on the trombone but had to be exiled to the barn to practice, plays the saxophone and lately has taken up the piano. Ann plays the viola in her local orchestra. Peter would have been so delighted to hear her play the sonata he wrote for her.

Nowadays I suppose we should have been discouraged from seeing one another since I was a student and Peter, a junior lecturer in the biophysics department. Fortunately in those well-behaved days, the perils of staff-student relationships had yet to become an issue: just as well, since we married happily and had five children.

But no-one has warned me that raising a family is such physical hard work. Life revolves around keeping up with the washing, using a 'copper' built in to the corner of the wash-house. I learn to wring sheets by folding them in half round the neck of the tap and twisting the ends together. Technological advances come in the form of a boiler and a mangle. Ironing, mending and the endless search to find a matching pair of socks take up any slack. We are hard up, living on grants which may or may not be renewed annually, in an old farmhouse that is falling to pieces and cold. In the days when the North Somerset coal field was still operating it had belonged to the colliery manager and there were three shafts in the field. I thought they were capped but found that one was not and the children were daring each other to clamber round its edge. We grow our own food, never quite winning the relentless battle with caterpillars, nettles and diseases. The plum tree dies of silver leaf and our dog snuffles her way down the row finishing off the raspberries.

We keep turkeys, rabbits and geese, and my oldest son Philip shoots the occasional pheasant which has had the temerity to stray into our field. Once we feast on jugged hare, so rich it exhausts even our appetites after two days. We import two or three goats, the idea being they will keep down the weeds. In practice they usually manage to get into the garden and munch their way through our precious vegetables. Englebert, a Nubian goat with long floppy ears makes a break for it, chewing his way from field to field through thick thorn hedges. I catch up with him eventually three miles away, sitting under a cider apple tree munching happily. I drive away quietly.

Followed into the house by a line of imprinted goslings, hatched on the central heating boiler, a visiting colleague of Peter's asks us if we do not sometimes feel under siege, which in retrospect just about sums up the situation. We are constantly on the verge of defeat by the natural world.

Our finances fail to expand as rapidly as the demands of a growing family and my craving for books. So I get a job, plenty in those days, just look in the vacancies column in the local paper and present myself for interview at the local mushroom farm. To the question as to whether or not I am over-qualified to be a quality control inspector, I reply that I think the interviewer overestimates the fascination of peeling potatoes.

My job is to count the number of maggots in representative tins and if there are too many, divert them from the Canadian market to the home market, a real conversation stopper at dinner parties. The job itself is incredibly boring. I stick it for a year, then start to read job column adverts again.

The nearest on offer is in Farleigh Hospital, at that time still reeling from the impact of the first of the big enquiries into mistreatment of 'people with mental handicap' as they were then known. My interview is brief. The head of the department calls me in and announces she has to go to a meeting. I say 'Goodbye'. That's it. I've no idea what I've embarked on and am astonishingly naïve.

At the end of my first day I'm told to return Charlie to his ward. As soon as we leave the day room, Charlie grabs a trolley and, using it as a scooter, sets off at high speed for the gates. Once outside he abandons the trolley and dashes up the hill towards the main road, leaving me trailing behind. A miracle happens – his pants fall off, and hobbled, he comes to a stop, waiting mutely for my assistance. At this point an entire career is balanced on a pair of faulty braces. I pull up his trousers and taking his hand say, 'tea-time, Charlie' and we set off back down the hill.

It is the proverbial steep learning curve with emphasis on control, physical if deemed necessary, and occasionally brutal. Possibly a legacy from the workhouse but it seems in keeping with large Roman letters painted blue and deeply incised into the stonework of the pulpit in the chapel, 'REPENT YE'. Grim.

Assisted by Dave who is overlapping for a week or so, I gradually begin to have some idea what I am doing. His parting shot is, 'Phoebe, you have to decide whose side you are on'. A timely warning since the rule appears to be 'do not disturb the status quo'.

Hostility stems partially from protective practice and partly from resistance to change and inertia. There is a general failure to acknowledge the personhood of 'the boys' as they were known 40 years ago. 'Thinks she knows everything' (support worker), 'Thinks she can change the world' (domestic) and most surprising, a warning after a couple of years from a consultant not to be 'too successful'. I am so shocked by the latter that I still find it difficult to believe. I do not even query what he has in mind.

Meanwhile my job is to 'look after' eleven extremely disturbed men in 'The Corridor' and to keep them quiet. This passage has a door at each end and is used as a shortcut from one part of the hospital to another. People pass through slamming the doors. Each man sits at a desk and has a box of broken toys to occupy them. Chairs and tables soon start flying in all directions and when the tempo rises too high, two of them respond by ramming their hands through the windows. Their arms are covered with white scars. Forty years ago, very little was known about how to relate to people with this level of distress. Watching this happen, I have no idea what to do.

I start by trying to find anything that will capture the attention of an individual – and in some respect this is still where I begin. I enlist their help to scrub down and then, begging paint, decorate the wall by each desk with a real life-size scene drawn from their lives. So Charlie, who had been brought up in a pub, has a bar with brass handles, and a buxom bar maid. He leans against her bosom to listen to her heart. Dave's father was a greengrocer, so the backdrop to his desk is a grocery, complete with boxes of fruit and vegetables he helps me to print. We borrow clothes from the laundry to dress the grocer standing in its doorway. When the shop is complete, he informs me solemnly that his dad's peas had maggots in them. Raymond loves trains, so I make jig-saw puzzles from train posters, with pieces big enough for him to handle. He sits by me as I cut them out with a jig-saw and inserts each into a tray. This is a man who the newspapers have described in animal terms and as needing four men to hold him down when he gets upset.

One day, hotly pursued by its owner, Raymond brings me a rose tree in full bloom he's torn from a flower bed belonging to one of the nurses and presents it to me huffing and puffing with pride. Blood and earth run down his wrist. It's one of the most selfless presents I have ever received.

His gift opens up his mindset for me. Rather than see him from my point of view, someone whom perhaps I can help, I see a gentle man with an independent viewpoint who is capable of planning in order to achieve his aims. It opens up his mindset for me. We talk so much about equality and valuing people but it rarely translates as being alongside each other. Look carefully. It's no longer about me doing things for him, no more 'Lady Bountiful', but about attitude and finding a way to share our lives and what we feel.

And how did Raymond know about red roses?

From these men who become my friends, I learn what it really means to value the essence of a separate person in their own right and to be honoured by their trust in me. Five of them start to use speech. They start queueing outside the door in the morning for me to open up. Word gets around and teachers come from local schools and then from further afield. Eventually the approach I'm using comes to the notice of the Norah Fry Institute in Bristol University, and in particular to its director, Oliver Russell, whose unsung skill has nurtured so many professionals, setting them on the way to use talents they hardly knew they had to the advantage of people with disability. Oliver arranges a Joseph Rowntree Foundation Fellowship which enables me to travel and study good practice and teach. Best of all, he introduces me to a psychologist called Geraint Ephraim who introduced the approach now known as Intensive Interaction. Gary is my supervisor for the next four years. From him I learn to use body language to tune in to those who are having difficulties with speech. Perversely, he also starts me off writing, since the only account he left to posterity is a small pamphlet with limited circulation. I now have ten books published and a number of films, snippets of which can be seen on YouTube.

'You sound posh.' This accusation comes from the back row of a recalcitrant group of support staff, whose main reason for signing up for training is that it offers a day off work on the wards. Difficult to counter, we do not choose our circumstances and I'm not prepared to feel guilty about mine. I can only do the best I can with what I've got.

But it's a long journey. I am so innocent – I think that all I have to do is be nice to people – but this is a blinkered vision and I've yet to learn that, autistic or not, the reality we share, our experience of the world, may be completely different. What I enjoy in sensory terms may be extremely painful for the person whose attention I am trying to engage. Lesson one: each of us is the centre of our own universe, the 'me that is you' is different from the 'me that is me'. This is so obvious, and yet, coming from a relatively privileged background (hard up mostly, but rich in substance), I need hanging up by the heels and rattling to take on board the implications of its veracity. Lesson two, which is related, comes from Bruno Bettelheim. Although one may not agree with his right-wing views, I totally subscribe to his point when he says that in working with autism, 'love is not enough'. We need to know what we are doing. And this means shaking off our own perceptions. What we see, feel and hear is not necessarily the same as that of the individual on the autistic spectrum. The imposition of our reality on them can cause them extreme distress.

From the point of view of engaging with people with autism, it is only recently that we are beginning to understand that distressed behaviour (I will not call it challenging since this implies a deliberate choice to harm another), is underpinned by sensory hypersensitivities. To take a very simple example, a patterned top worn by a support worker may set off painful visual distortions, more than just a disadvantage in the current obsession with black and white clothes. Everyone from the newsreader on TV to high street shoppers is wearing zebra stripes in one form or another. When the visual effects of this become unbearable, a man in a day centre tries to pull the T-shirt off his key worker. Interpreting this as a sexual attack, I am asked if they should send for the police or psychiatrist. In response to my question as to whether he does it when she is wearing a plain T-shirt, they say, 'no'. What he is saying by his behaviour is, 'please do not wear that shirt as it hurts'.

This same type of response can be triggered by auditory hypersensitivity, when a particular frequency (usually a high pitched one in a hard voice) sets off enough pain for the child to attack the speaker – most often their mother, since the problem is usually to be found in a woman's voice. Switching to a low soft voice is not easy, since how we use our voices reflects our personalities. Nevertheless, if it can be managed the aggression comes to a stop.

Failure to understand the sensory problems experienced by children on the spectrum is very often built into their environment, particularly the architecture of schools. New-builds tend to go for glass, bright lighting and echoing high ceilings. This looks terrific on the planning board and opening day but can have disastrous behavioural consequences. Children cannot attend to their teachers or learn if they are fighting off anxiety and pain. Fanciful additions such as portholes in the wall for children to look through, can terrify a child who is struggling to understand their boundaries.

I've been trying for some time without success to find a way of talking to architects and those planners who draw up the specifications for new schools, so it's with great pleasure that I received a booklet called *Aldo goes to Primary School* written by a firm of architects who have been drawn into researching the problems placed on autistic children by unsuitable environments[32]. This is a really helpful book and needs to be read by all planners. Gail Gillingham sums it up when she says, 'children on the spectrum need visual and auditory tranquillity'[33]. We need to measure what we are providing by these standards.

The Joseph Rowntree Fellowship lasts for four years on the road. Since I am a widow and my children are dispersed, I lead a nomadic life, visiting schools and hospitals around the country, teaching and learning at the same time. Improvisation is a help – an entry class for children with profound disability has been trying to save up enough money to black out a sensory room for years: black plastic silage sacks do the job in an afternoon. I suspect health and safety would prohibit this solution as a fire hazard nowadays but we arranged them so they were temporary and could be taken down easily and put up only when supervised. Meanwhile the children had what they needed.

One of my greatest joys is working with a man with autism, Adam, who desperately tries to get hold of black plastic sacks and will break into furniture if he suspects there were some inside and eat them. An x-ray shows his stomach to be chock full of bits, including a long length of plastic coated wire. He attacks staff who

---

32 McNally H, Morris D, McAllister K (2013) *Aldo goes to Primary School*. McNally Morris Architects.

33 Gillingham G (1995). *Autism – Handle with Care*. Tacit Publications, Inc, Edmonton, Alberta, Canada.

try to prevent this behaviour and is on four pages of medication to stay his aggression. His staff nurse and I think perhaps he is eating it in order to keep it, since otherwise his bits are taken away from him. We decided to bring him to my workshop (black sacks hidden away safely). Using power tools hands on – he loves the vibration – we make a sizeable box to keep his plastic in. We fill it with black sacks and carry it to his bedside. Now he has no need to eat his plastic. An month later an x-ray shows only one piece in his stomach. But there is more. Two years later when I visit the home to which he had been moved, Adam spots me across the lawn, dashes over and leads me by the hand up to his bedroom and proudly opened his box. It is full of plastic rubber balls. He no longer needs medication. The manager told me that every now and then he would take out the balls and organise his fellow residents into playing games. All he needed was somewhere he could keep the things he treasured – not much to ask.

Then until now: you know you're getting old when you get asked to be an Honorary President. Today one such invitation arrived accompanied by a purple T-shirt, embroidered in rainbow colours with the logo, 'Us in a Bus'. Underneath in white letters are the words, 'connecting people' and in larger letters, 'President Phoebe'. I'm not sure I shall ever have the face to take off my sweater, but am truly proud of it. It means a lot to be asked to be associated with such an effective team working with people with autism and other disabilities.

Peter dies young. I am bereft.

Half mad and beside myself in grief, I sit on our Emperor size mattress and try to cut it in half. It seems logical at the time – I shan't need it any more. However, unable to reverse the timeline with a small pair of curved nail scissors, two or three snips are enough to convince me that this is not a practical option.

Only my youngest is still at school. I sell our rambling ruin and move into a small cottage in the same catchment area.

Work continues, with individuals, in group homes, with parents and schools, with social services and the NHS. I make films, teach, growing a reputation that no longer requires I advertise, work comes to me, takes me around the country and sometimes abroad, particularly to Denmark and Sweden. 'Workshop Contributor' graduates to 'Principal Speaker'. Growing old, the Sternberg Prize for people over 70 who are contributing most to the community takes me to Downing Street (No. 11 not 10, although we all have to have our photographs taken in the more famous doorway). Bristol University awards me an honorary degree for work on communication with people on the autistic spectrum. In love with the dales, I move up north, followed eventually by Margaret. Which is where I am now.

Even without the ancestors, this life story rehearsal is taking far too long: maybe I should just stick to DOB, 11.07.33; that indispensable date without which access to banks, health services and other life support systems is a non-starter. And of course my mother's maiden name. What happens when I can no longer remember it? I need a mental Ctrl and F.

I needn't have worried about the length of my life-story, since my interrogator has yet to come back to record my wanderings.

Sitting room

Ten days after Peter's death I meet the father of one of my children's friends out shopping. He shifts uneasily from one foot to another and finally blurts out, 'Getting used to it then?'

At present I'm floundering in the search for company and belonging, a quest not easily satisfied and highlighted by the frequent enquiry, the nature of which reflects the speaker's need for reassurance, rather than a disinterested desire for information: 'Settling into the new flat then?'

While a rhetorical question doesn't require an answer, there should be an alternative word for a query with a specifically preferred answer ('yes' in this case): one that excludes a prolonged whinge about getting old and existential aloneness. So I give them the affirmation they want – but it's like picking at a scab that is trying to heal but is still leaky. I know I should confront the pain but it's slippery and difficult to get a grip on its amorphous shape.

So, whether I like it or not, it comes back to the competition in our lives between needs of self and that of belonging and contributing to a social group. What happens if one feels oneself to be an outsider?

(Smile at yourself in the mirror, smile and give yourself a squirt of endorphins.)

But I thirst for shared humour, for psychological fearlessness, for the trust that grows from creative relationship. Even so, finding and negotiating the early stages of friendship is risky, although we can shorten the odds to meeting parallel minds by finding spaces which reflect our own interests. Likely haunts for such encounters are places that attract oneself; we are creatures biologically designed to seek mutual support in company.

When Peter and I kept geese (76 of them), the flock organised itself on the basis of triads, two geese to one gander. If there was a surplus of ganders, they isolated themselves on the hill and stopped eating. Broken hearted or self-sacrificial, they simply starved themselves to death. That is except for one pair, for whom gender turned out to be less important than mutual support. They sensibly adopted a homosexual partnership, alternating the roles of male and female.

Restless still.

Perhaps the most pressing component of present unease is that I am still awaiting the DVLA's decision on driving. In an attempt to etch their beauty and tranquillity into permanency I try and assuage my desultory agitation by day-long excursions into the dales.

Yesterday I followed the tree-lined lane that wanders beside the stream up Garsdale to the viaduct, drove on through Hawes to my favourite pub for lunch – it was full up, nowhere even to park. I turned away reluctantly and, laughing at myself, ate a fairly nasty lunch on sticky tables in the nearby farm-shop. Big mistake to try and organise perfection.

In view of the problem of loneliness, it's ironic that, apart from the practical difficulties of shopping and such, the greatest deprivation of being unable to drive would be an inability to get in the car and drive into the hills – the freedom just to get away and be alone.

However, psychological survival suggests that we need to distance ourselves from bad days. Some years ago I was introduced to the concept of 'Boo' days and

'Hurrah' days, a popular term for Emotivism[34]. While it has its critics, Emotivism proposed that ethical statements express emotional attitudes rather than propositions. Instead of being swallowed by inevitable disappointment, I learned to stand back and acknowledge the affective quality of my reactions to transitory events – and ask myself whether my emotional response was commensurate or over the top. (Detachment does not always win; I should make a poor Buddhist.)

Today I'm driving along a stretch of road where, years ago, I passed a crashed Mini, squashed by impact almost to the size of a tea crate. No interior space. A naked arm, hand flung wide open, stuck out of this box from a slit that must have been the driver's window. Just metal and flesh.

As I drive by this car crash site now, it seems bizarre that there's no trace impressed on the tarmac, bank, field, hedge and hill. I recall that after the war, my father took me to an exhibition in London featuring the ruins of Hiroshima. I saw the shadow of a human limb burned into a paving stone. He said, 'I want you to remember this'. But now, on this roadside, the plastic wrapped bunches of flowers have been taken away – there's no blue plaque to commemorate the nurse who died. No fissure in space says a timeline stopped here, on this carriageway, violent death took away life. There remains only my personal graffiti scribbled on the walls of affective memory, still registering horror.

So, today is a Boo day, bad but not bad enough to allow the lorry wobbling across the road in front of me to terminate my lifeline. In a way, the question that needs to be resolved is simple, I need to find friends, like minds, people to talk to. Not easy when you are old. A meeting of the University of the Third Age looks promising but enrolment day is a nightmare; 300 or so

34 Ayer AJ (1936) *Language, Truth and Logic*. Dover Publications.

people in a tiny hall shouting at each other. My head literally begins to swim. There is no writers group, so I scribble my name on the psychology list and I retire as quickly as possible.

It's true that the world is waking up to old age and the need to make provision for it, but in the rush to redress what has been disgraceful care, the pendulum is in danger of swinging too far. Now the emphasis is on activity and a happiness that does not take account of failing knees and stiffening and aching bones. The paper that plops through my letter box, *My Times*, is a celebration of old age, complete with photo montage of a white haired couple holding hands and leaping into the air like a couple of teenagers celebrating their A-levels. My personal experience of old age is that it is not 'whoopee'.

An introductory photograph of the editor of this misguided and patronising pink and blue missive suggests she is in her 40s. My neighbour and I agree she has a lot to learn. Some of the articles are interesting – but its Saga presentation reads like a toothpaste advertisement, complete with devastating smiles, glossy teeth and no sign of shrinking gums and dark cavities. It makes me feel like a turtle-shaped curmudgeon about to withdraw into my shell.

Since people live behind closed doors, I'm not sure that chance encounters in the lift are going to assist in the task of meeting people. Proactive measures seem to be demanded, a broadcast policy that reaches out: filtration can come later.

I discover my wheelchair-bound neighbour likes fruit, so instead of the standard cup of tea we share a bowl of cherries. Black, succulent, and nearly as big as plums, we spit out the stones and swap stories. We both lived in Watford during the doodlebugs (the limit of their range) and shared bangs: the dawdling engines of any that reached that far, cut out and fell.

And an unexpected door opens up as a result of having entered the Langcliffe poetry competition in a neighbouring village. Unable to get to the fete on the day due to stomach pain, I'm invited to collect first prize, an enormous purple and green shield, as big as my monitor. Not sure where to put it but the presenter turns out to be fun, and suggests we meet for lunch.

She tells me her idyllic village is embroiled in a vitriolic row, the kind that flourishes in small communities like bugs in a petri dish. A new owner of the big house has served notice to quit on the allotment holders, on the grounds that their activities disturb her tranquillity and she does not like the look of the sheds. Mini-diggers arrive and plough up their vegetable plots, subsequent rain washes away the topsoil leaving a sea of mud. Needless to say, a number of the entries to the poetry and short story competition relish the opportunity to lampoon her misjudgement. However, the judge was generous in his assessment of my effort:

'It is a wonderfully evocative poem full of delightfully vibrant and original imagery. The verse has a superb sense of place. Langcliffe is vividly realised by a poet who clearly has a deep understanding and love of this part of the country. I so much enjoyed the very clever structure of the verse, the contrasts and the power of the language.' Gervase Phinn.

In the quest for people to converse with I realise most of my friends are artists scattered round the world and I wonder if this is vicarious – a failed painter swinging on the coat-tails of those who have made it – but I dismiss this idea. I should rejoice if I had their skill but know enough about myself to understand that liberation from the concrete to the abstract is not achieved without much trawling of the 'undermind'[35,36], combined with a particular singleness of purpose. More importantly, my own work with people involves deep plunges into intuition and insight, and as much energy as I can muster.

To be fair to myself, it is affect that grabs my attention and draws me into friendship, rather than the personal struggles of an artist manqué with her inability to translate what is in the mind onto canvas. So perhaps it's time to resume the promenade and look at the pictures in my sitting room.

I am a collector by nature. On my travels I've been a magnet for beautiful things. Not necessarily expensive, each artefact in this flat has meaning, there's nothing here that is unrelated to the life I have lived, am living. If my memory is episodic, this display is the affective timeline that mounts the postcards. The difficult part has been not only to select what has the most meaning but also to hang it so that the walls do not look cluttered. Each offers a starting point to reflection.

Some years ago, I spend a fortnight with some friends in the Australian Bush. One day I ask to be left alone while they go off down to a river to explore. I sit on a rock by a small stream tipping over a cliff, overlooking a vast and prickly landscape. Used to looking at containable landscapes, this is a world without end. Orange hornets about three inches long, drone around in the scrub. Otherwise there is a stretched and hazy silence – and as the day wears on, heat. It becomes clear that I have to find shelter. The only shade offered is a narrow shelf with a crack along its base. As I turn and move towards it, my eye just catches the movement of a long black and white tail

---

35 Claxton G (1998) *Hare Brain Tortoise Mind*. London: Fourth Estate.

36 Gerard R W (1946) The theory of gravitation only when the metaphorical apple falls on the prepared mind and the process has reached some threshold level. *The Scientific Monthly*.

curling into the darkness. Choice: snake, lizard, goanna or death by heat stroke. We snuggle up together.

So my first picture in the hall is a print by an Aboriginal artist. *Guambayi* is a great black snake wriggling through grit. Signed William W, its vigorous contortions fill the frame and represent both creature and its journey – and in this respect it reflects what we all present to the world, individuals honed by our experiences. Bought from the only gallery run by indigenous artists themselves, the picture is one of a pair. Moving through into the sitting room, the second is a reflection on Cyclone Tracy that laid waste to Darwin. The eye is sucked into a whirling black hole. Both these pictures use the original earth colours and vibrate with power.

Quite different and yet one of my favourite pictures is a blurry abstract print of the child's game, noughts and crosses, which summarises the misty ambiguity attending most of our lives. This and the print beside it are both by Philippa – a few straggling lines suggesting a tussock of grass, or possibly a derelict snow fence beaten down by the wind, such as one sees tottering by the lonely road linking Ribblehead to the Wensleydale.

Hanging by the window is an oil painting of Park Fell, backside of our local mountain Ingleborough, on a wild day. The composition is interesting, a wall drives straight up the middle of the canvas into torn cloud. By all the rules of composition it shouldn't work, but it does, brilliantly.

The left hand wall is lined with bookshelves, divided in two by a Romanian cupboard. About twenty years ago, the Romanians decided they preferred MDF kitchens and sold all their handmade artisan furniture. (The pinewood is weathered almost grey and has to be supported by an internal framework.) Between the bookshelves, its top is a perfect plinth for *Gabriel*, a tall serene figure sculpted by Peter Eugene Ball using driftwood and bronze. One of his wings appears to have been momentarily ruffled in a breeze and sticks out but the archangel is unperturbed. When I ask Peter where he finds such interesting fragments, he says the best area for beach-combing is along the English Channel after a storm, where boats have been wrecked on sand banks left behind since Doggerland was breached by rising sea levels after the last ice age, submerging the land bridge linking England with France.

The kitchen in this flat is through an arch. On one side there are two more prints. The first I brought back from Hong Kong. Rather than the typical Chinese souvenir of a galloping horse, I wanted a picture by a contemporary artist. In pictorial terms, this abstraction is difficult to explain but is about multiple personalities, as if the boundary between me and not-me is a semi-permeable membrane, through which we can diffuse different facets of our self to engage with alternative people. If not consciously, we all do it.

Hanging below this, Lorna Graves lies asleep underground while her dream animal roams the world above – and on the other side of the arch, a wonderful painting by James Martin, *The Creation of the Birds*, is lavish with gold and blue. An angel sweeps past a flowering tree, watched by a peacock-like bird, scintillating.

But I have left until last the watercolour by Norman Adams. It hangs tucked into the corner, facing away from the light, so its colours will not fade. This is a painting that makes me laugh, the Newcastle Bridges drape like necklaces across the bosom of the Tyne: road, rail and pedestrian costume jewellery combine to link murky shores.

My sister once introduced me to a game which involved viewing a landscape through the eyes of a particular painter. An easy one to start off with is to visualise oneself standing in London with one's back to the National Gallery looking down Whitehall through the eyes of Canaletto. Not so difficult; the architecture lends itself as backdrop to little groups of brightly dressed people gathered in Trafalgar Square. Now switch to Lowry, take the colours down a peg or two and the groups have separated into drab rush hour individuals, each hurrying home, lost in their own world. How about Salvador Dali? Icons melt, Nelson's column droops like a faded tulip, Marble Arch is on its knees.

Back on my walls, humour, power, intimacy, abstraction, each picture is not only decorative but unpacks rich stories that broaden the horizon, introducing new dimensions to my personal perception. My appreciation is not exactly possessive – over the years they have become an integral part of who I am, so that even if I were to lose them, they are embedded in my psyche.

Interval

One arm of a rainbow stretches down from inky cloud, slicing the Warrendale Knotts. Sheep dipped in prism graze at the pot end. (I admit they are too far up the hillside to distinguish such multicoloured detail, but it's a nice idea.) Ephemeral, the rainbow lasts just for a few seconds before the cloud and sun shift their relative positions – deleting both vision and fantasy.

Up and down: Boo and Hurrah days are behaving like a treadmill that hasn't made up its mind which direction it is pursuing. The pendulum is overreaching its arc. What lies beyond the edge of the earth? Stephen Hawking is suggesting that if we fall into a black hole, while our corporeal self will disappear, our energy and information may emerge in another universe – albeit in a slightly garbled version[37]. And we can't come back. Sounds a bit like death?

Meanwhile, Hurrah. Determined to make the most of my (possibly) last driving days I take the high road from Pateley Bridge up to How Stean Gorge and over the fells to Leyburn. The view is spectacular – heather moorland just coming into flower and the Yorkshire plains stretch away beyond. A winding reservoir divides the hills. Flowers line the walls. Denim blues fade into the long line of the Yorkshire Moors. At the north end, it is just possible to make out the lopsided triangular peak of Roseberry Topping.

---

37   Merali Z (2014) *Stephen Hawking: "There are no black holes"* [online]. *Scientific American*.

Boo. On the way down to the Yorkshire Plain
I reverse the car onto the verge to allow a tractor
to pass in narrow lane. Bang. Back tyre blows. The
tractor is well away over the hill and I'm alone in
the middle of nowhere with a cuckoo, no mobile
signal and (the latest space saving innovation in
new models), no spare wheel. The hole in the tyre wall
is big enough to thrust a couple of fingers through.
All I can do is bump along slowly and pray the hub
doesn't crumple.

Hurrah: man in a shed – the sort of shed that is
buried under piles of discarded tyres and a layer of
oily grime you can smell a hundred yards up the road:
a miracle in the shape of an agricultural engineer,
proprietor of an old-fashioned garage who actually
mends or makes parts, rather than sending away for
spares. He says don't worry, he'll fix it. Can't find
hub nut key so he lies on the floor and drills it off.
(Presumably thieves can do the same.) I sit in the
front seat eating my picnic while he searches the
county of Yorkshire for a new tyre. Coils of pressure
tube dangle from the hooks. An extended row of
spanners, from the size of toothpicks to the weight of
blunt instruments hangs along the walls.

Man returns with tyre. Back on the road and so
much for the cuckoo.

Boo: my computer has crashed. Hurrah: the DVLA
is five more weeks behind with paperwork, voice at
the end of the phone suggests I see my doctor (whom
I've never met since the one who interviewed me has
retired), to advise (Boo). Hurrah: oculist says my eyes
are well within the limits for driving. Boo: IT expert
can't come today – teaching tomorrow and need
screen for showing films to visiting student. Hurrah:
in an unusual burst of confidence, revisit computer,
replace SCART plug hanging out at the back.

Hurrah again: Court Manager sends message to Housing Association he will ring the police if they don't fix toilet at once as it is a health and safety issue. Plumber number eight, arrives, no change. (In Paris, after a Dutch firm has given them the sack, eleven pi-pi ladies are picketing their toilets outside the Sacre-Coeur with daily demonstrations.)

Note to Manager:

'Although it did not catch on at the time, the first toilet was designed in 1596 by John Harrington and he installed one for his godmother, Queen Elizabeth, at Richmond Palace, although she refused to use it because it made too much noise. Enough time has elapsed since then to get the system working effectively. Since most are not decorative articles of furniture (although the avant-garde artist, Duchamp got away with one as a work of art), all I want is a toilet that flushes adequately. Maybe we should arrange a Parade with Protest Banners to coincide with Official Opening of the Building on October 1st?'

I rather fancy hanging a sheet from my balcony daubed with 'FIX MY LOO' in large red letters.

The consequence of this proposed 'fix my loo' demo is a stiff message from the Manager of the Housing Association indicating that there are 'proper procedures' to be followed. Plus advising me that plumber representative number nine is on his way and should arrive promptly.

Tomorrow is today. Charming man, head of design, looks down the pan, completes standard test flushing away 12 sheets of loo paper, agrees mine is not fit for purpose. Discussion about tank volumes follows, 2 ½ or 4 ½ litres, (a couple of pints?), eco-friendly but inadequate heads of water. He also admits that this is an 'antique model' with an old-fashioned pull the chain system. Direct action for ever! Best wishes to the pi-pi ladies.

Snakes and ladders

I have a home-made in/out system on the ledge outside the front door, together with 'Please do not disturb'. It would work perfectly if I remembered to change the card when I leave or return to the flat. I am the flaw in my own choreography.

Time to take stock:

Firstly, it's difficult to record what has happened over the last six months without trespassing on individual confidentiality. Looking back, I've tried to follow roughly the train of events as seen from the point of view of this end-user.

In practical terms and as a result of resident pressure, things are moving, deficits are gradually being addressed. The manager has checked with other residents and it is now acknowledged that (in spite of the builders being in denial), the water did actually cease to run when the electricity went off during the thunderstorm. There is nothing so hollow as the suction of a dry tap. Apart from the possibility that in the clumsiness of old age candles might get knocked over, he is also concerned that given how the supply tanks are linked up, the safety of drinking water might be compromised. (Presumably it also establishes my credibility and I am cleared from suspicion of geriatric fantasies.)

So I email a poem to the Court Manager, which he forwards to the Housing Association, together with his suggestion that the Grand Opening be postponed until the building defects are addressed.

Teething Problems

The Flats are lovely but there are
flaws in the retirement home,
taps that run dry in thunderstorms,
lightening water cuts,
how do residents smother flames
climbing from a spilt candle?

The Flats are lovely but there are
structural anomalies, spy holes
and a fan switch too high to switch
or spy, tepid showers –
and pans that fail to pass on
evacuation, an automatic door
that bites. Technicians, plumbers
come and leave, fiddle
with chips and circuits, replace
valves, disappear – the residents
gave up on notes to the office
and proper procedures some while ago.

The Flats are lovely but radical solutions
are still-born in the birth-pool of intention.
what we need to know is when
remedial intervention will fix the systems,
preferably before Open Day?

Political lampoon presents an awkward marriage
between external circumstance and the intuitive
burrowing and groping that precedes pen to paper.
Although this is doggerel, I like the idea of stillbirth:
it was written to nudge things along, with humour
as lubricant.

The next response is a visit to each resident from
a representative of the Housing Association enquiring

in detail about outstanding building defects. She tells me that it is the first time she has heard the water/electricity story and that she will investigate it immediately. 'The Grand Opening with Big-Wigs' (so described by a member of staff) has been put off until the defects are addressed. Hopeful date is January. Instead, a super-inspection by someone who I take to be a chartered surveyor, undertakes a meticulous examination of the cracks in my plaster and notes them down.

Close up on the home front, a few more nudges and the steering committee of the Residents Association has been recognised by the Housing Association. Agendas are beginning to be couched in more co-operative language. I haven't really done much in my role of Hon. President except try and persuade people to listen to each other. Have decided to resign since I don't think they need me. I haven't the energy to cope with the machinations and don't go for figureheads.

At a personal level I don't seem to have a lot of luck meeting people through U3A, University of the Third Age. The prospectus assumes everyone knows where they meet, so I end up wandering through the rain looking for them in the wrong street. When I ring her, the tutor tells me that they don't actually know much about psychology so the course is in the nature of an exploration, aided by a university course for beginners: sounds a bit vague. Appointments clash and work takes priority. I can't manage the next date, so the course will have to be jettisoned. And this is the trouble, I do find myself too busy or tired to take on extra commitments.

These last ten days have been chaotic: Glasgow (training), Keighley (urgent call from parent), Warrington (two days assessing five children) and finally, on Saturday, a day's home tutorial with a student psychotherapist from London.

After she leaves I get up early and look out of the window. Morning mist clings to the Warrendale Knotts. The sun is rising behind it, its brightness both expanded and diffused in a muslin cloud. Soon, heat will burn off the moisture, but for the moment its incandescent flare is cold-brilliant, I can't look anywhere near this quarter of the sky. A student emails me a photo she took before she headed back south: we were both held in this white blazon at the same time.

But everything is hanging in the balance since the DVLA still have not got back to me with their verdict as to whether or not they will renew my licence. I'm trying to be grown-up about this but my guts are not responding to the idea of detachment – gastric juices are gnawing their way through the stomach lining. It occurs to me that the Licensing Authority will probably have difficulty catching up with my records since, as I moved, these are in the process of being transferred from one hospital to another and I gather this may take months.

It's difficult to think about anything else at present. I try distraction in the form of a day trip to Cartmel Priory which advertises itself as having a 'Magna Carta celebration and flower festival'. The Magna Carta turns out to be a copy, the priory is heaving with people and the flowers are wilting.

Swallowed by the snake again, this one takes me back to Start.

If one is as lucky as I am, people are kind, reach out to you, arrange things for you, tell you when this will happen, that will happen, or fix things for you – or they do it themselves because it is quicker and they are never quite sure if you have taken it on board. I am grateful and at the same time resent being treated like a child, even while acknowledging that in this internet world I am less competent than most three year olds texting their way through their social lives. Catching a train to London, I brood on a city transformed from a cluster of villages, each with its own identity and texture, to a sprawl of skyscrapers and unloved terraces bought as investments, an urban jungle with too many people and too much noise and dirt, a city that has sold its soul to celebrities and oligarchs laundering currency. In general, body language is that of avoidance. Last time I was here I saw Madonna getting out of a taxi and walking up the steps to her new house. She was wearing beige and looked intensely bored.

It is even difficult to recognise myself, let alone where I am among anonymous concrete shells. When I was a student, I walked daily from Kensington to Bloomsbury dodging offers in the park. Every street was stamped with its familiar facades and smells. I felt connected. I even remember the acentric shape of a paving stone that has survived the blitz. A dog had been sick beside the bus stop outside the block of flats where I lived 76 years ago. Now that I am reduced to a head-down struggle against pedestrian flow, I feel displaced, a pebble shaken in an empty box. I don't belong here. It's not mine any more. Why should it be? The London I know and love is in the cupboard, a past sell by date carton stuffed with recollections.

With work it's difficult to keep abreast of demand, which is exponential. One can plan all the arrangements so carefully and silly things happen – in Liverpool to give a seminar, the speakers have been stolen (not surprising in that particular area), so no sound. Equally so in London a couple of days later, when a young man fiddles with the set-up during lunch: again, no sound. Twice in one week. It's hard enough without this sort of irritation since the films are sound dependent – my only consolation is that in neither case was the problem caused by my technophobia.

I feel like a wimp but have just turned down an

invitation to talk to the Chromosome 18 European Conference in Rome (at 83 I think it is all right to say I'm not up to it). Last time I spoke to them was one of the highlights of teaching. A lad in the front row started to make sounds which got louder and louder. Rather than speak against them I decided to use them to show the audience how effective it could be to communicate through response to body language. I was able to tune into them. The room filled with people clapping to our rhythms until it seemed like the whole hall was just one person, a dance in unison, over a hundred people having a ball. It rose to a crescendo. He was so pleased he got up and took a bow.

But it was difficult enough getting to London and back. And the temperature in Italy in August is liable to be close to 40°C and I'm no good in the heat. Although I should have delighted in the opportunity to speak at an international conference, a colleague will do it for me. Janet, with whom I've worked many years and who runs a service for children in London, is just as competent a speaker as I am. It makes the idea of letting go easier.

Returning home after a week away the dreaded DVLA buff envelope has arrived, enclosing a request that I retake a modified version of the visual field test. Chin resting on a cup, look straight forward at the central light and press the buzzer whenever another light flashes. 'Twinkle, twinkle little star, how I wonder where you are', because after a while the brain is liable to panic and produce dim flashes all over the place. How many shots in the dark am I allowed before I shall be accused of cheating and escorted from the department?

Surprisingly polite and intelligible, the letter explains exactly what I needed to know in simple language. This time, instead of testing the eyes separately as they do in the ophthalmology department, both eyes will be tested together.

Since I don't drive around with one eye shut, it seems a more achievable option. I should be able to pass since I've been using the fire alarm flash in the ceiling to run a similar test and can scan the whole visual field with both eyes wide open, one compensates for the other. If I fail I shall know that I truly have a blind spot and it will be easier to accept.

My post is full of stars. Fired by success in the poetry competition, I enter and forget about a competition run by Settle Stories to write a story called *My Journey to the Stars*. The catch is that it has to be written on the back of a post card. First prize is to have a heavenly body of some sort named after oneself (a rather larger prize than the poetry shield, but convenient for display without requiring house room). I fancy this and toss off a quickie first-person account of defrosting after a cryogenic journey, to find the rest of the crew dead in their pods. Sadly it doesn't win but the judges like it so much they create a second 'special prize' of two tickets for a show I can't go to. Should have preferred a very small satellite fragment of rock whirling round in space, a dedicated thumbprint on the void – would have enjoyed such a tenuous connection with the cosmos, even if unable to place it. And think of the naming ceremony, champagne broken over a telescope?

When I was about five – and all the world was still strange – my sister Prudence woke me up, took me by the hand and led me out into the night to show me the Milky Way, that mysterious chiffon veil of four hundred billion stars, a galactic disk of which we are an infinitesimal part. She was a member of the Royal Astronomical Society, one of a vast army of amateur star-gazers who explore the darkness in search of un-named lumps of rock. She would wrap herself in blankets, lie out for hours in a deck-chair with her binoculars trained on a particular quarter of the sky and record meticulous observations in a ledger. Perhaps it is all done by computer now but at the time these professional amateurs were responsible for many new findings.

More stars, or rather planets this time. While I was away I stayed with Ann, my second daughter, and my grandsons, Jamie and Steven, came to lunch. Clever lads, Steven is a software designer working on a system for the the Probation Service and Jamie (following his great grandfather, who proposed a solution to the problem of the vortex while waiting for a train and watching a steam engine), is a cheerful mathematician working on the design of a rocket. His calculations are aimed at ensuring that the heat generated during landing does not burn up the nose cone. As his father Tom says, we shall know who to blame if the module fries millions (billions?) of pounds as it hits the barren wastelands of Mars.

Why bother? The interstellar reality is that if our species is to survive the inexorable decay of our planet, we are going to have to build another ark and send a few bold representatives into the unknown. Meanwhile, space travel by genetic proxy blows my mind.

Here, I am aware of my size, both minuscule and without end. In one of her films, Donna Williams talks about the difficulties her autism posed to developing relationships[38]. She sees other people as paired up, able to cluster – but she can only be a visitor, 'which is all right if you like to travel'. Infinity wipes the boundaries set around imagination and I am a child in my space ship. Brrm-Brrm.

Come Thursday, no sign of plumbers.

Update (time and date important enough to be specified). Never mind how many electricians it takes to fit a light bulb, eleven plumbers later, on the Tuesday,

38 Williams D (1995) *Jam Jar*. For more information visit http://www. donnawilliams.net/jamjar.0.html

4.30pm, 10th of November in the year of our Lord 2015 (about a year since I first looked at the flat), a ring at the door announces the arrival of the Court Manager (and plumber) clutching a the large capacity tank. The Cover-the-Stud-with-the-Palm-of-your-Hand flush mechanism works by shading the plunger from light – until the batteries run out. The advantage is that this model will continue to operate during a power cut. The downside is that the batteries will require changing at an unspecified date: memo to keep spares and a bucket handy.

It's curious that after seven months running battle, the installation itself is something of an anti-climax. Ricky, from Rotherham, empties the old cistern for the last time, connects it to a suction pump to remove the remaining drops, apologises for the noise it makes, removes a few screws and replaces the small tank with the new one: simple, no champagne flush, nothing remarkable. We should have had a band and some fireworks – disappointing in a way and leaves a hole behind, a space that was occupied with equal measures of irritation and black humour, one that I'm not sure how to fill. Until of course, the batteries run out over a bank holiday weekend.

Need not have worried about the absence of something to worry about – now the weather is turning cold I try switching the underfloor heating on, only to find that the bathroom floor remains cold. The contractor informs me that this is because I have set the thermostats incorrectly (it's my problem). As with earlier faults with the shower (tepid but corrected by the turn of a screwdriver) and the curious incident of the lightning strike that turned off the water as well as the electricity, denial seems to be the default position of his department. In this case, repeated complaints bring in an outside plumber who informs me that the heating controls are wrongly wired up. The latest defect is that the intercom system has stopped working, so that my unattended visitors are stranded on the far side of the security door. Am I to suppose that I this is also my fault? In a home for the elderly, it is so easy to shift the blame onto fading brains.

If it were not so farcical, I should feel angry. No. Anger is a slippery customer and once launched it latches on to any handy dissatisfaction. Turn the page.

But I am angry: angry at the incompetence of systems and the refusal of individuals to take responsibility for deficit; angry at my personal failing capacities to deal with these and splashing out; angry at our 'me-orientated' society where, egged on by the fashion industry, it is thought acceptable to spend £3,000 pounds on a bag to take on holiday (truly) and yet cannot afford appropriate provision for its most vulnerable members. Our children are brainwashed to focus on style and which celebrity is wearing what. Where have our priorities gone? Collectively, we have lost our way. It is unsurprising that there is rebellion against such materialism.

So why don't I sell everything I have and give it to those in need? Although in financial terms, it would not amount to a great deal, and I do respond to a number of the appeals that appear on my doorstep, this question has me wriggling like a worm on a hook. Good intention founders on the rock of self-interest. I don't want to look at it.

Settle

Freezing morning: I lie in bed recalling my school days during the war. (Heating was subject to the whim of a capricious generator. Frequently when we woke, our flannels were frozen hard. We used them to hit each other.) How quickly can I get through this morning's ritual of dash into the unheated bathroom, pee, clean teeth, strip, wash and get out again before my toes turn blue and fall off? Why not just stay in bed under my warm duvet? There is actually no reason why I have to get up. But the undermind has been busy overnight and in the end it is words and stumbling ideas that get me out of bed. Half-formed sentences trip over on the threshold of consciousness. If I don't write them down they will be gone.

Moving into sheltered living is a one-way upheaval. In order to accommodate myself to the change, I not only need to meet people but also to familiarise myself with the place where I live, to flesh out and embed myself in my surroundings. I want to add the dimensions of geography and history to my environment, to know where I am in every sense.

My generation is easily identifiable. Apart from our sagging and papery flesh, we are dependent on 'aids', leaning on anything handy, wandering round the aisles of the supermarket hugging the basket of our trolley (using it as a kind of thoracic surf board). Since walking is not easy, getting about is no longer a pleasure.

Clutching an assortment of tourist guides supplemented by internet excursions, explorations need to be selective, preferably of short duration and on flattish terrain.

Not easy to achieve in Settle, since the streets are not only hilly and in places cobbled, but the pavements, which periodically narrow almost to extinction, camber sideways and deliver the unwary into potholes and gutters: very picturesque but demanding for the aged.

Settle is an ancient limestone town in North Yorkshire, crowded between the massive overhanging crag of Castlebergh Rock and the young River Ribble. Our sheltered housing block is separated from the town by a large car park. On the left, a tree-lined alley leads to the Post Office. If you walk straight on, a small one-way street leads past Liverpool House (so-called because of its proximity to the turning point for the proposed link to the Leeds-Liverpool canal) and some cottages towards the market. The Liverpool connection is interesting since cotton for the mills was brought from there, and presumably tobacco for the snuff mill, although little evidence remains of this trade apart from the name of one of the mills as Snuff Mill, or T'Owd Snuff.

Now that information is so readily available on the internet, a tour of the town runs the risk of sounding like a guidebook. But Settle oozes history, the past cannot be avoided, although the town does somehow manage to avoid being quaint. It is intriguing rather than charming. Perhaps this is because it is rooted in rural industry. Its buildings are four-square, solid, pragmatic. Its indigenous inhabitants are farmers, dealers, engineers, people who fix things, make the world go round: supplemented now by retired walkers, climbers and cavers who fell in love with the dales and never went home. There is a strong Quaker element centred on an early Meeting House.

The market square is bordered by the Shambles
– and on the opposite side, a café, The Naked Man,
complete with much photographed plaque, whose
private parts are delicately concealed by a 1663 date-
stone. A partially cobbled road leads up from the north-
east corner to The Folly, an elaborate but structurally
dubious looking seventeenth-century private house:
wrap-around windows embrace the corners of the
building, seemingly to place an unbearable weight on
their mullions. A friend who is a chartered surveyor
looked at it and muttered, 'more money than sense'.

The Folly doesn't feel like a good place to be sheltering
during an earthquake, although apparently it survived
a two-minute shift in the Craven Fault (or possibly the
Pendleton Fault) in 1944. Not only did chimneys fall but
'people leapt from their beds and much alarm was felt.
Furniture rocked and window panes vibrated.' Some
people thought it might be an air raid. One resident
dashed to the window, expecting to see surrounding
houses in flames. Many farmers reported they could
plainly hear the rumbles moving along the ranges of the
hills. A local vicar (presumably an ex-naval man), likened
the noise to a torpedo passing under his house.

The cart-wide lane behind our architecturally
unlovely block of flats climbs steeply through stone
cottages towards Castlebergh Rock. Some of the cottages
have their original roofslabs. Thick as a man's two
fingers, I stop to ask a roofer what they are called. He
tells me they are known locally as 'greys' or 'sandstones'.
The roofs bend under their weight. Further up, at the
base of the cliff, an information board is tacked to a
loosely swinging gate. Torn from the 1720 notebook of
Samuel Buck, a pencil sketch is indistinct and does not
match the accompanying text, which describes a crag
face laid out as a sundial, 'huge slabs of rock with the
hours marked out on them running down the side of

the hill'. Presumably this was in a period when not all the population had access to time pieces: enterprising, although it might have been more helpful if the sky was not so frequently overcast in Settle. Sadly, the hour-lines have eroded and there is now no sign of them.

Behind its glass, the poster is mossy and blurred. Closer inspection with a magnifying glass reveals that the scale of the picture is quite different from what I had first taken it to be, turning out to be a distant sketch of the town and its surrounding hills. What I thought were scratched graffiti on the cliff face are the small cottages climbing the slopes.

As a visitor some years ago, I walked up the path to the summit rock with its flagpole. Now largely derelict, in Victorian times this area was developed as a pleasure garden with swings, a roundabout and hobby horses provided for recreational purposes. (Given a hobby horse in my early childhood, I wasn't sure what to do with it. An anachronism from an age when horses were the work-engines, it was a toy that needed to be dragged around rather than sat on like a go-cart, unwieldy, bump-bump-bump, no speed in it.)

Entry to the gardens was 2d for adults and a penny for children. An 1820 photograph shows sedate women in cartwheel hats posed on the swings. Probably having to hold their breath in order to remain frozen in time, there is no sense that they are enjoying the exposure.

Further along, a second notice addresses present dangers and carries stern warnings regarding the instability of its rock face. Overgrown steps are cracked and slippery. A disclaimer from the town council warns that no liability is accepted for loss, injury or damage. BY ORDER. In particular, visitors are advised not to sit, or stand below the crag while it is being climbed. Beneath its shadow, rooms at the back of the old chapel, now for sale, are deemed to be at risk.

Nemesis looms over Zion.

Most of the buildings in the centre of the town were rebuilt in stone around the 17th century, replacing the wooden and thatched houses that were a fire hazard. Bound by river and hill, new-build expansion is geographically limited to the south and south-east. The houses are still mainly limestone, ageing from an aggressive ochre to softer grey, the colour of an old sponge; which in a way is what it is, being derived from calcareous shells deposited in shallow seas. Sadly, our flats are built in composite stone which is unlikely to weather. Together with their useless Juliet balconies, not even wide enough to hold a decent size plant pot, they may never blend into the landscape.

Apart from the Castlebergh Rock, Settle is also famous for its railway station, a basket of ironwork and begonias, presided over by a helpful station master who is happy to negotiate his way through online timetables and any number of connections. On days that steam engines run, the Settle to Carlisle track is lined with railway twitchers. Cameras at the ready, they aim to catch the perfect shot of gleaming engines steaming across the Ribblehead Viaduct, whose 24 arches soar across the valley between the back end of Ingleborough and Whernside, before tunnelling under Blea Moor. Built for the Midland Railway by Irish navvies, the men and their families camped in shanty towns thrown up by the side of the advancing track. Odd bits of rusty tool and rail still surface from the peat. Over a hundred people died during construction, many from industrial accidents but more from small pox. Graves of the workmen and those of their families are to be found in the nearby churchyard of Chapel le Dale. (From the sublime to the ridiculous, one snowy day I wait two hours clinging to a tree on a rocky knoll overlooking the small stream that runs beside the cemetery, while a camera man from Saga struggles with his lighting equipment to get the perfect shot to accompany an article they are running. Modelling is not my strong point, I look very cold.)

The railway opened to freight traffic in 1874, followed by passenger trains soon after. The famous viaduct is very exposed to wild winds: nearly a hundred years later, several brand new Humber cars blew off their wagons and landed on the ground by the viaduct. Imagine them tossed like autumn leaves by the wind as they floated down into the embryo Ribble – there was a missed photo opportunity.

My favourite visitor attraction lies between the station and the viaduct. A siding to the east links the main line to the remains of Hoffman's lime kiln, an extraordinary industrial ruin, roughly the size and shape of a battle cruiser.

Bending low at the top of a flight of steps, one enters a dark and mysterious chamber which loops round a central block of furnaces. Each furnace served a burning chamber stacked with limestone blocks and coal and sealed by a temporary wall. While that chamber was fired, the adjacent one was filled. When firing was complete the wall was torn down and lime shovelled through an arch into waiting railway trucks outside. It took six weeks to get round the circuit. Working conditions, particularly during removal of the hot fired lime, were appalling. The air was full of burning dust.

The kiln fire ran non-stop from 1893 to 1931. When I first visited it many years ago it was almost forgotten; enquiries at the tourist information bureau were met with blank looks, they did not know of its existence. Today it is refurbished. The men who worked here speak from information boards:

'They knew how long it took to burn it see, before they advance the fire, happen a day and a half to two days, gradually they move the fire forwards. They knew how long it would burn at a certain heat.' (Ted Ramsbottom)

'That was the worst job of the lot was the lime drawing, particularly in hot weather. Ooh I've seen them come out fair blistering. Used to drink a lot of beer did them chaps as well.' (Fred Pollock)

But tucked away as it is at the base of the huge quarry, this remarkable ruin still has few visitors.

Inside, daylight through the arches gives the appearance of being inside the nave of a cathedral, with window strips of light curving away into the distance. Flues are nesting places for bats. Rare hawkbits climb the walls to the crumbling roof. During the war, the space was used for storage. It's spooky: my grandchildren loved to play hide and seek in and out of the doorways.

Rising under the shadow of Whernside, the tallest of the three peaks, the River Ribble runs downstream parallel to the railway towards Settle, diving head first into Stainforth Force and over a weir on the way. A very small ammonite is curled asleep in the rock beside the fall, one of the only ones I have seen in these parts.

Kayaking is popular. Recounting the hazards of trying to shoot Stainforth Force, a paddler describes the hollow behind the waterfall into which a canoe can easily be sucked and the difficulties of escape.

'What most people don't see is the large undercut cave that exists behind the curtain of water that forms from the bottom drop. A 'Double Stopper' exists which if you happen to end up in would be very difficult to escape. The cave goes back a considerable distance so beware of getting looped back into the fall. If in doubt have a look in dry weather. Best of luck.'[39]

Settle is around twelve miles from the river's source

---

39 Andy Plummer (2013) *UKRGB The UK River's Guide Book*. River Ribble Helwith Bridge – Settle

and responds rapidly to heavy rain in its catchment area, streams swelling from meandering trickles to urgent torrents: deceptive to the extent that, ignorant of an upstream downpour while on a school outing, two children were swept away and drowned by surging levels while exploring an apparently harmless side stream in Stainforth.

Where I am standing, a footbridge crosses the river just at the point where the great slippage known as the South Craven Fault has abandoned a gigantic limestone rock in the water. Known as Queen's Rock, this mossy and slippery lump is part of a shallow cascade on a slight bend. Trees line the bank and paisley patterns of bubbles swirl slowly in the surrounding pools. Not surprisingly a favourite spot for Victorian picnics.

Between the Ribble and the town is a modern industrial estate, occupying much the same site as the manufacturing cotton and snuff mills of earlier times. Some of the remains of these buildings are visible, particularly Kings Mill which has been converted into expensive looking flats.

How far can we go back in time? In Attermire Scar above Settle, bones of hippopotamus, rhinoceros, elephant and hyena dating from 130,000 years ago have been dug up from the floor of Victoria cave. The first actual evidence of people is a Mesolithic harpoon point made from antler horn. The Romans used the cave as a workshop.

Nowadays, history is at the business end of a metal detector. A friend who lives locally took it out for the first time into a neighbour's field to search for a ring he had lost. Buried in the earth he found, not the ring, but a length of metal, about a foot long. Whether for fighting or for hunting (and as yet undated), it is the carefully shaped head of a formidable weapon. Poised on the edge of becoming an exhibit slotted into local history, this spear was an essential part of the original owner's life support system. However corroded, being able to shake hands with the past in this way, is a metaphor made literal and immensely moving.

The settlements of Giggleswick and Settle grew up around a ford across the Ribble. Before roads were built in order to get to Kendal, the centre of the snuff trade, the traveller from east to west would have followed pack-horse trails across the great bulk of the Pennine hills before having to negotiate what the Ribble Paddler described as a 'double stopper', that is descent of the steep crags of the South Craven fault and then fording the river on a track now known as Kendlemans Road, at a place just a little further downstream from the footbridge. Any trail further south would have got bogged down in water meadows and marshland. The crossings could only be made when the river was reasonably low, so there must have been a long wait sometimes in the winter.

Cross the footbridge into what now appears to be a satellite village of Giggleswick – but over time, the two settlements have swapped importance. Originally Giggleswick was the dominant settlement, with Settle as part of its parish. The Domesday Book, in which both appear, records Settle as having a taxable value of six geld units and Giggleswick, nearly three times as much at seventeen geld units[40].

Around twenty years before that England was in turmoil. William the Conqueror had invaded the south but was contested in the north by a coalition of Saxons and Danes centred on York. Known as 'The Harrying of the North', his response was brutal. Not only did he burn

40 A geld relates to the tax raised to pay off the Danes when they raided, levied at the rate of two shillings per hide, a hide being the area of land under plough sufficient to support a peasant and his family.

the villages and slaughter all the inhabitants between York and Durham, but history records that he also salted their fields and smashed their ploughs, so any survivor who was sheltering in the woods died of starvation.

Less often quoted, William also laid waste to large parts of Cheshire and what is now Lancashire. The question I've been unable to answer is how he moved his troops from east to west. Did two separate armies march up from the south, or did those in the east cross over the Pennines using existing trails and possibly ford the Ribble at this juncture, where I am standing now. Certainly Craven cannot have been unaffected, since there can have been little food following the massacres. And, although retribution was indiscriminate and did not necessarily imply participation in the rebellion, the Lord of the Manor of Giggleswick was replaced by one of William's allies. Roger of Poitou (William's cousin and advisor) added Giggleswick to his extensive holdings, although subsequently he forfeited this when he backed the wrong horse in a rebellion against William's son, Henry II.

On his death bed, William is alleged to have said, 'I persecuted the natives of North England beyond all reason. Whether nobles or common, I cruelly oppressed them: many I unjustly disinherited: innumerable multitudes, especially in the County of York, perished through me by famine and sword... I am stained by the rivers of blood I have shed.'[41]

Being on the right side (the winning side) was largely a matter of luck and accident of tenancy. During the Civil War, the Royalist Cliftons of Skipton held the manor – but, unusually, their tenants in Malhamdale, who included John Lambert, did not follow tradition and tow the line, becoming instead a Parliamentarian General in Cromwell's army. In 1651, his troops camped in Settle on the way to encounter the Royalists in

41 Orderic Historica Ecclesiastica books iii and iv.

Lancaster[42]. In an effort to re-centre myself in time past I reflect that 364 years ago his soldiers were probably milling around here, just about where I'm standing. Not all that long ago, about five of my lifetimes.

Settle began to grow in importance when, in 1249, Henry III granted the town a Market Charter to be held on Tuesdays, which it still is. Today I bought fish and eggs and a fake-fur quilt for my bed – a bit slithery but light and warm. Independence as a parish was sealed in 1838 when Settle built its own church. In springtime, the churchyard is a froth of snowdrops.

Past and present live side by side. Two jet trainers interrupt my historical excursions, swooping up the river valley between Whernside and Ingleborough. I cross back over the stone bridge and turn left into the car park of Bridge End Mill, converted to flats in 1986. This block of flats overlooks the weir and salmon ladder. But what has brought me here is the Archimedes screw with its hydro turbine, capable of generating 50 kilowatts of electricity and linked by cable to the flats. Surplus power is fed into the grid. Any profits are donated to local charity. Brilliant – and straight back to the classroom.

I'm around eight and looking at an illustration of an Egyptian farmer (or more probably his slave), turning a treadmill attached to a large screw to lift water from a ditch onto dry fields so that his crops will grow. The man is standing sideways in the conventional Egyptian pose, which makes his anticlockwise task look awkward. Presumably he would be standing face on in the field. But what sticks in my mind, is the idea of farming in a harsh environment, the possibility of taming the desert and using natural resources to improve the quality of life. Archimedes is said to have cribbed the idea from the Egyptians.

---

42 http://www.settle.org.uk/history

Leaping back from the third century to the twenty-first, the screw is reversed and now powered by the river. Channelled through an original mill race, water stumbles over stout fins, spinning the shaft. Installed in 2009 after some considerable wrangling with local anglers who predicted it would mash the salmon swimming upstream to spawn. This fear appeared to be justified by a drop in salmon numbers – but actually coincided with a national fall off.

Set in its place, this is no lightweight fan. Its statistics reinforce its seven ton solidity. The screw is massive, tilted at a shallow angle of twenty-two degrees and capable of twenty-seven revs per minute.

However, even though there is water in the river today the blades are not turning. Peering down through the heavy protective metal cage, what I see looks like a conch abandoned by the tide: there is no perceptible movement at all. Perhaps I know so little about the workings of an Archimedes screw that the movement is meant to be imperceptibly slow? Or maybe the project has died of natural causes?

Disappointed, I turn back towards the town and under the high arches of the Leeds-Settle railway line, towards the market square. On my left is a steep road up to the doctor's surgery (you need to be fit to be ill in Settle). At this morning's early appointment I am initiated into the process of blood pressure selfies: place your arm into a sleeve which inflates and delivers a print-out.

While the tourist board does a good job, information about a place is only half the story. However illuminating, facts leave us out of sync with history. The same riverbed still fills: we are here but still a witnesses on the bank, not swimming in the current. In spite of all our efforts we can never know how it felt. It would be simple if we could insert the passages of time into a machine and receive an affective reading.

Nevertheless, 'knowing the facts' shapes how we look at our environment. It's the soil in which we root: there is a 'here' to be in.

I'm not finished with the screw yet: need to know more about it and about the people who conceived this green initiative. Is it really dead? Enquiries lead on the one hand to Wikipedia for photographs, and on the human side to an old-fashioned haberdasher's, stuffed with wools, ribbons and craft materials. The owner suggests I ring her husband – he started the project. I'm swept up by his enthusiasm and buy a single share, £200, on the basis that I shall not get the money back (profits go to charities such as mountain and cave rescue) but will be contributing to a local project. I suppose one could call it buying into the community but it feels good.

Today is glorious. The crag is swathed in a mantel of copper and bronze autumn leaves shining after rain in the sun. Reasoning that, as I usually manage half the distance, at least I can get there, and so I walk down to the river. Coming back can look after itself.

I was wrong about the demise of the hydro – but its operation is constrained between certain water levels. This time the river is in spate, a mean muscular animal. Now that I'm a one-share shareholder, I want to see the Archimedes screw in action and here it is, propeller churning away vigorously. The sturdy blades clunk through the steel mesh. Potential to kinetic energy, water to turn on the lights: literally powerful, feeding the grid.

We live on energy. Recently, my son Philip came home from the jungles of Papua New Guinea where he has spent the last twenty years extracting gas from the highland forest, a similar transmutation and one that the local villagers took in their stride. They told him they were not in the least surprised that there was energy under their mountain, since their sun clearly grows tired during the day and retires under one side of the mountain in order to rest, recharge and come up reinvigorated the other side the next day. During the time my son has been there, the story seems to have been embellished a little since it now runs to a codicil about a man who came from afar and lit up the mountain.

What is interesting is that, in a similar legend originating in Egypt (and creeping up across the European landmass to Scandinavia), the sun stands on a pedestal and rides across the sky in a chariot during the day and sails through the underworld on a boat by night. Relics of this legend are to be found in Bronze Age rock carvings, particularly in Scandinavia, together with cup and ring carvings. Juxtaposition of the carvings suggests that the sun is the cup and the pedestal is the post that supports it. Remnants of this belief are to be found in the cup and ring carvings in Northumberland, and one or two on Ilkley Moor near here.

Egypt and Papua New Guinea are a long way apart from each other so perhaps we at looking at coincidence, after all, it is one way of interpreting the relative movements of the earth and sun.

When I was working in Sweden I was taken to see similar carvings in a dammed river bed. To reach them we had to walk out over a gantry coated with ice. A notice warned that on occasion the dam would be opened and an alarm would go off: 'If the klaxon sounds, RUN'.

Meanwhile, I have to get back from the river to my flat and it seems I've miscalculated my personal energy resources. So I stop and rest every hundred or so yards – wherever a handy wall or seat presents itself, including one in the middle of a motor-bike rally. I sit down firmly and announce that I am after a souped-up quad bike. A big man in sweaty leathers comes over and moves his jacket and an empty plastic cup up the bench and gives me a sympathetic grin.

The last lap home is across the car park, a long flat area the length of the Rugby pitch, the original turning point for barges on the abandoned branch of the Leeds-Liverpool canal. Time for a pause, or perhaps more to the point, time pauses: half way across the park I stop to reflect on the discontinuity experienced between an 'instant delivery' pace of modern life and the slow-down of an elderly brain that enjoys reverie and leisurely footfall. Imagine being able to synchronise the rhythms of old age with the unhurried lap of horse-drawn barges.

Car Park

The old woman pauses by the recycling bins
for rest, for reflection.

Before the Leeds-Liverpool canal
ran out of funds, this car park and pitch

would have been the turning pool for barges;
she would have had space

to sit and think – or just sit –
watching horse-power churn the water

dozing on the wooden benches,
as the long-boats turn, head back to port.

Which, given the time-tabling of local buses that take off at a tangent into the countryside and abort, might actually have offered a more speedy mode of transportation than is currently available. As far as trains are concerned, Lancaster and Leeds are still running on a War of the Roses timetable – red and white rose stations separated by a mile and no direct route between them.

The business of transport is still very much on my mind at the moment since I took the DVLA driving test the other day and made a horrible mess of it. The test machine was different from the one used in the hospital and for some reason my mind superimposed the requirements of the previous one onto the one I was trying to get to grips with. Red and white dots flew in all directions. Not used to panicking, I was completely lost – can only wait and see but I should not have passed me. The tester sticks to her script, calling after me, 'Have a nice afternoon'.

So now my attention is focusing on how I shall manage without a car. A fellow resident lends me a catalogue of mobility aids. Leafing through its pages it is evident that one can spend a lot of money getting old. From rugged all-terrain scooters, tilting beds and tip-up chairs to expedite movement or repose, discreet commodes (to avoid embarrassment), walkers, rollaters, reachers, frames, handles and grab-bars, to beakers with a nose 'cut-out' (to enable the user to drink without tilting the head) and toothpaste squeezers for those with limited squeezing capacity – ingenious solutions to cater for every infirmity.

In spite of the manufacturers logo – a scooter doing wheelies – my attitude to aids is one of ambiguity. While they may help to maintain independence, they are in themselves badges of decrepitude. I should be grateful to the creativity that has gone into the design of these props, but they are icons of deterioration.

I suppose that my ingratitude is a question of pride. In this hilly countryside one can get away with a walking stick – but yesterday I bought a second one, elegant, light weight, adjustable height and extremely strong. Used together, the pair take the weight off my pelvis in particular, away from that point where a screwdriver is actively drilling its way into the joint

– and I can walk more easily. Nevertheless, such an improvement feels like a step downwards towards the carpet-slipper shuffle of the rollator. Perhaps the trick is to focus attention on the goal rather than enfeeblement; what I want to do rather than the image I present. And as my wheelchair-bound neighbour tells me, when she slept so badly that she had to summon help six times in order to relieve herself, one gets beyond humiliation.

There are so many factors involved, loss of independence top of the list. What of work and distant friends? No more pottering about in book shops – and wandering around junk and antique shops. (Probably just as well since lust has clearly outrun shelf space.) Then there is getting food and reaching dentists and the mundane activities that make up the ordinariness of life. How quickly one slides into the foreshortening that accompanies decrepitude, house to flat, through progressively smaller areas of engagement to wheelchair, and of course that ultimate box: nailed down at last, no more gadding about in one's coffin.

Journeying

Journeying

'Journeying' is a word invented by a delightful small boy to describe the comings and goings of his family in relation to the activities of The Caldwell Autism Foundation, which his father started in order to promote the use of body language as communication – 'are we going Phoebe journeying again?' It is these journeys and the teaching and interactions that are under threat if I cannot drive; in practice, my whole way of life and possibly my identity. This is what I do, this is what I am. The stuffing of my mind is autism.

Yesterday I drove back from Glasgow after working in an assessment unit, one day seeing individuals and the second teaching based on what I had learned the day before. It is a filthy drive, starting while it's still dark, with so much water on the road that all the lights double their reflections in puddles, making it extremely difficult to pick out the signboards, especially just south of the Clyde where three motorways merge in a short distance. Getting into the right lane is tricky enough in broad daylight, let alone before dawn. Edinburgh, Stirling, Carlisle? It is really a matter of luck when I find myself driving south into the snowbound Lowland hills, rather than east or west.

But Glasgow is an easy place to get lost in, especially as they keep tinkering with the motorways, so I think I know where I'm going but end up somewhere totally unknown. The first time this happened is some years ago, around midnight and pouring with rain. I am very late because the trains from Edinburgh have been suspended and the only way is by road – a journey that should have taken an hour lasts four. I manage to come off the motorway into what seems to be the red light district. Women huddle in doorways while their pimps hover nearby. Hopelessly lost, I pull up near a woman and enquire the way to Sauchiehall Street. She looks at me pityingly and says, 'Yer canna get to Sauchiehall Street from here'. She's correct, although it is less than a quarter of a mile away – road works form an impenetrable barrier between where I am and where I need to be.

The second time I get lost in broad daylight, when I follow signposts to what I think will be a quicker way to the motorway and lose myself driving round and round a circular route somewhere in the eastern suburbs. I stop and asked a lollipop lady for directions. She replies that she doesn't know but points me in the direction of the next lollipop lady several junctions ahead. And so I progress from one lollipop lady to the next, until I come to one who tells me that her husband is parked round the corner and he will tell me how to escape.

Getting lost the third time is on the trip from which I have just returned, when I find myself driving out as far as Prestwick Airport looking for a junction that exists on my map but not on the motorway. Coming off and stopping to ask a builder, he peers obligingly into his smart phone and, turning it round, announces that he cannot help me as he does not know where we were at present. An older and less technically dependent man gives me explicit directions immediately.

The obvious answer is to join the 21st century and use Sat Nav, but apart from technophobia, I am reluctant to do so for a number of reasons. The principle one is that leaving A and arriving at B is the dull bit

– what is interesting is the context, the castle over the hill, the history and geography of journeying, a three dimensional sense of where I am in relation to my surroundings (or not, as the case may be). And in our increasing dependency on guidance systems, this instinct for place is rapidly getting lost. Like the young man trying to be helpful with his iPhone, ask someone to show you where you are on a map and they haven't got a clue. Even a funeral director standing in his shop door in south Manchester could not tell me where he and I were at this time. Somehow one would have thought that (especially) an undertaker needed to have a clear idea of his territory. One would not want to end up in the wrong place.

It may sound exaggerated but even if we can choose its gender, we are becoming servile to a voice (not always accurate), losing a hard-earned dimension, our instinct for navigation, reducing our skills. If we allow our right (intuitive) brains to wither at the expense of the left hand interpreter, we do so at our peril. (During the war, all signposts were removed so having a good 'bump of locality' was deemed essential.) And next time I am lost in London and unable to stop and consult my map in fast moving traffic on a dual carriageway, I prefer to know that if I keep the sun over my left shoulder, I am driving north and will eventually hit the M25. It works. Adventure is getting replaced by risk assessment, so, 'Hey, for the open road', even if it's the wrong one. And besides, without getting lost, I should never have encountered the delightful Glaswegian lollipop tribe.

Accommodation has its hazards, from pillows that reek of pomade (no, the management have no spares), to the notice in a bedroom: 'Residents who spill tomato ketchup and curry sauce on their bed linen will incur a fine of ten pounds'. A fire alarm goes unanswered by the woman who pops her head out of the door of her room and announces she is not responding as she needs to take out her curlers first. Perhaps the most astonishing reaction is on a ferry returning from the Outer Hebrides when the sevenfold siren sounds, 'Whoop, whoop, whoop....!' Nobody moves. Looking up to the Bridge, the Captain is frantically running around trying to find a button to switch it off. Perhaps this is a regular hazard so local passengers greet the alarm with inertia?

I try and arrive at my destination the day before working so I can rest and gather my wits. If I have been asked to find ways of making contact with individuals, I don't want to read endless reports on their 'challenging behaviour', rather than how they are trying to communicate: it's easy to pick up a negative image which can colour assessment. When we meet I want to see them with fresh eyes, as they are today, now. And since some are highly disturbed, I want to make contact with them using body language before I invade their personal space.

Some of the children and adults I'm asked to see are very distressed: occasionally people ask me if I am not afraid. This is interesting because it raises the question of what it means to be brave.

Perhaps some people are so charged up with adrenalin that they are literally fearless in the face of danger. Others are afraid and continue. In the 1914-18 war, my father was chief test pilot at Farnborough. One of his most spectacular contributions stemmed from the need to protect planes from the lethal effects of flying accidentally into hostile balloon cables. In a strategy to counter this, he modified his plane by stretching a wire from the nose to wingtip and deliberately flew it into a dangling cable. On the appointed day, the weather was bad and his test-flight had to be postponed. For days he waited for possible conditions. In a diary he describes his apprehension. On the third day he took the plane up and flew into the cable. Instead of tearing the wing off, his plane went into a spin from which he was able to pull out just before hitting the ground. He was the only test pilot of his time who survived.

To get back to myself, on the courage scale I rate myself as timid in the face of the unfamiliar – and yet, although I may be nervous in anticipation, once engaged I am so locked into the body language of my partner that I'm not aware of self, only of the dance of interaction, the response, the give and take, the 'being with' rather than 'doing to'. For this reason I try and discourage the natural instinct of staff to make a formal introduction such as, 'come and say hello to Phoebe', which puts us in the wrong modality with regard to each other. Rather, I will listen, a listening with all my senses, to the feedback they are giving themselves. This is the doorway, the porthole, where I can get access to what has meaning for them. The other point to remember is that my partner is almost certainly more scared than I am and it is their anxiety that is triggering their defensive behaviour.

In practice there have only been two incidents when I've been attacked badly and in both cases I made the mistake of overconfidence as a result of initial success. The first was with Dai, a man who, driven to distraction by the painful sounds in the small and overcrowded dining room, would go to his room after breakfast and beat his head against the wall to try and rid himself of the perseverant noise for up to ten hours. If interrupted he became severely aggressive. Attempts to modify this behaviour had proved unsuccessful to the point at which it was proving difficult to get anyone to support him.

Using Dai's sounds empathetically I was able to reduce his distress to the point at which he had come out of his room and was sitting quietly downstairs. Not listening to the instinct that was warning me he was not ready yet, since I had to teach in about ten minutes, I tried to move in closer to him and got head-butted hard for my insensitivity. Nevertheless the manager was so impressed by the way his anxiety had drained away that he said he would try this technique of tuning into his body language. I replied that in addition he had to be sure that Dai had breakfast in a quiet place since it was the sensory overload that was triggering his distress. Following this advice, Dai was restored to calm.

Which brings me to the problem that when we try to address disturbed behaviour, the question we are so often asking is, 'what do we do about this now' (containment), rather than looking for a proactive solution, 'what is the underlying sensory trigger to the behaviour and how can we modify this?'

For example, some people on the spectrum find certain frequencies in the voice unbearably painful but are completely calm if we speak to them softly, or in some cases introduce them to special acoustic noise reduction headphones. Designed for helicopter pilots so that they can speak to each other over the engine noise, these ones cut out about 80% of incoming background noise.

But, as with all burgeoning relationships, our responses need to be intuitive, responding to the present moment, understanding when we are in accord and being prepared to withdraw if we find ourselves treading on sensitive ground. All of which makes it difficult to take on approaches that require the drawing up of a set of rules as to how behaviour should be modified. Our interactions are not about doing X,Y and Z, but about individual response to the child or adult's affective state, their feeling status as expressed through their body language. And because it is about relationship, each individual in a dyad will have a different way of meeting their partner's communications, however they are displayed. Each of us has to learn the language of the other and respond to it in our own way.

Another question I was asked at a seminar given at the Royal College of Psychiatrist's annual conference was, how did I 'know' that a particular behaviour was linked to a particular trigger. Again it comes back to intuition – and intuition can be wrong. We can only find out if our supposition is correct if anxiety is reduced and there is behavioural change.

At a dinner in Cambridge in a famous college, I am seated next to an eminent biologist who asks me what I do and, before turning his back, tells me sternly that as a scientist he requires more empirical evidence. Suitably crushed I am left to contemplate that Intensive Interaction is not so different from the scientific method (which was drummed into my university ears), building a hypothesis and testing it, with the outcome that, in this case, if you get it wrong you will get thumped: just anecdotal evidence at the end of a fist.

Arriving home (note HOME) I unload the car and trip over a large pile of post that has accumulated during my absence – including two manila envelopes. Although they do not spell it out, there is something ominous about them. This is it, well at least I managed to get to Glasgow, do a good job and get back in spite of the weather. From now on my life is going to be different. I sit on the edge of my bed, reluctant to open them, wondering if I should rush out and do some last minute shopping. Eventually I tell myself to get on with it and tear open the flap.

I have been such a big idiot; made up my mind that I had lost my licence and worried myself sick as to how I could continue to work and carry on with the life that has so much meaning for me and is, to some extent, my identity. But here it is, the little pink card and God bless the DVLA who have given me another year, after which I can re-apply. Astonished, I sit holding it for some time, wiping its plastic faces with my thumb, running my fingers round the four corners to feel if it is real. It's here, it's mine. Life can go on. I ring Margaret and we talk about how, after I had taken the test to which she had taken me, I had been in tears, was literally falling apart, so convinced was I that it was hopeless. (Although I do have to say that there is a small part of me whispering that, after a drive as hard as yesterday's, I did wonder if not being allowed to drive could have been a blessing.)

Back here, Christmas is coming (it has been since July in some of the shops). Overnight, the town hall has donned a decorative silver foil tutu, coyly covering its first floor windows. Flaunting my driving licence I have no need to think myself into being geriatric for at least another year. This is my home and I like it.

Umwelt[43]

Although its eye is over Iceland, storm Desmond has emptied months full of rain on the North West overnight. The car park is flooded to the point where the wind is whipping up waves. Coincidentally or not, a section of the cosmetic boundary wall has fallen onto the pavement revealing its shoddy construction, no through-stones to tie the two sides together, the sort of higgledy-piggledy erection a child might throw up and knock down. One hopes that the walls of the flats are more structurally sound.

In the surgery a couple are waiting for their name to be called. The man has a raincoat over his knees. He looks puzzled, starts to pluck at its folds, 'what's all this for?'

Suddenly the reality of an ageing population is hitting the headlines. The papers are full of good advice, eat less, walk more, keep the mind active and, whatever you do, do not allow globules of fat to squat on your pancreas. Hindsight sees us in terms of failure. A just-turned-30-year-old celebrity offers advice on celebrating womanhood and embracing age.

Concern about dementia is re-enforced on the one hand by my bedtime reading – a fascinating novel that recreates confusion so powerfully that I find myself sucked into the mind of an old woman who has lost her

---

43 Much of this chapter uses as its starting point David Eagleman's inspirational book *The Brain: The story of you* (Canongate Books, 2015). 'Umwelt' is the German word he uses to describe the world as we see it, our personal version of reality.

friend and cannot convince anyone that her anxiety is anything but the ravings of a scatty geriatric[44]. On the other hand, and closer to home, a recent discussion with a friend about the music we enjoy. Although I can hear the tunes in my head, aside from the initials of their composers, our exploration flounders in the face of my total inability to recall their names. Fortunately we are in her second-hand book shop. She dives into the shelves: the Oxford Dictionary of Music comes to our rescue. Starting with A, I scroll down. Almost at once, 'Appalachian Spring' provides the necessary links – immediately my inner librarian knows I am looking for Aaron Copeland and his astonishing work, 'In the Beginning', a solo reflection on the book of Genesis.

Once when I was in Blackwell's Music shop in Oxford I asked the assistant behind the counter for a particular recording of this. After some discussion, she looked at me shyly and said, 'I once had the honour of singing the soprano solo', which expresses perfectly its ethereal beauty, so unlike the rest of Copeland's genre. His gallops across the pastoral and urban American scene are good-humoured but it is the haunting setting of 'the Lord God breathed into his nostrils and man became a living soul' that brings me to my knees.

Shaken by my inability to recall names (the information is still around inside but the inner network of links is eroding), I come home and sift through my favorite discs. Not having thought about it in this light before, I am somewhat surprised that all are choral works.

Extraordinarily, I first heard 'Dies Natalis' by Finzi when I was in labour with my eldest son. An infant sees the world for the first time – 'The corn is orient and immortal wheat, I thought it should never have been

---

44 Healey E (2014) *Elizabeth is Missing*. New York: Harper Perennial.

reaped or ever sown'. In Michael Tippett's 'A Child of our Time' the singer laments he has no money to buy bread. How shall he feed his family? Add in Elgar's 'Dream of Gerontius' and the powerful drumming in 'Akhenaton' by Philip Glass. When the Sun King dies, the priest intones his departure in a sonorous bass monologue – 'Open are the Double Doors of the Horizon'. The drawn-out echoing vowels are mesmerising; here is an invitation to walk into another sunrise.

Each of these works is a reflection on critical times in the condition of being human; what they share is solemnity and compassion. Looking at my heavy-weight selection of desert island discs, I note the absence of 'fun'. Not that it's not there but life is tough and it is rare. Laughter is a treasure to be nurtured, cherished and usually shared with friends.

It's time to recalibrate myself to the run-away pace of the internet. Life-changing ideas are evolving and disseminating worldwide at lightning speed.

The other morning before I leave Glasgow, I turn on the news to see if the weather is likely to moderate (no) and catch a programme about advances in modern technology, 'click'. In particular the neuroscientist David Eagleman is demonstrating a vest which uses cell-phone technology in the back to convert patterns of incoming sound frequencies into vibrations. These forward convert the proprioceptive input to electro-chemical signals to the brain, which the brain can then translate to information (words). His interest is in helping the deaf to decode a silent world. When I think about individuals who are unable to respond to sounds – but do find meaning in rhythm and pattern – it seems possible the vest may be of use to some children and adults with severe autism.

Back home, I tune in to 'TED Talks'[45] and here is Eagleman on TV, talking not only about aids for the deaf but also of the possibilities of expanding our sensory perception in new ways, of assimilating information in the form of add-ons. His talk hinges on the fact that the amount of information we are able to take on board is limited – our brains simply do not possess the necessary organs to take on board, for example, the echolocation possessed by bats, or the magnetic homing of migratory birds. With bodies that are transparent not only to email conversations in transit but a whole range of waves from infrared to x-rays and neutrinos, we are also insensible to these modes of information gathering since we do not possess the necessary sensors to detect them. David introduces the useful German word 'umwelt' to describe the world we perceive, as opposed to the actual reality out there. We assume that our umwelt is all there is.

Eagleman's work hinges on the fact that while our sensory organs pick up sound and vision and touch, each converts the stimuli it receives into electro-chemical signals – and it is in this form only that the brain receives incoming information. He points out that the brain is alone in its skull 'locked in a vault of darkness' and all it is interested in is figuring out what to do with these signals. So it should be (is) possible to transmit speech via a tablet to the vest and have its frequencies converted to a pattern of pressure signals, which are then forwarded to the brain in the electrochemical form it would naturally receive them. What the brain has to do is to learn to make sense of this data and put it into a form which automatically conveys the same information as speech. David likens this to the capacity of the

---

45 'Ted Talks' are introductions on YouTube to serious science delivered in simple language for the non-specialist. They deliver mind expanding ideas to the unversed. Amazing.

Braille reader who obtains information directly from
the raised dots on the page without consciously having
to work out the meaning, rather than having to wrestle
with each letter, word and sentence.

Receiving information in the brain and
understanding how to make use of it are separate
processes: our sensory perception does not come
naturally – we have to learn how to use the input we
receive. Perhaps this is what we mean when we talk
about the innocence of childhood, a state where our
sensory intake may appear beautiful. (Finzi's Orient
corn had never been reaped or sown but had occurred
out of itself. Without needing reason, it just was.)
Untempered by context and experience, our brains have
yet to grasp how we may fashion such impressions to
our needs.

Learning to use our visual and auditory intake is
linked to proprioception. An interesting (but bizarre)
experiment contrasts two kittens being rotated
horizontally in a cylinder with vertical stripes on
the wall. One is contained in a sleeve, the other has
its limbs free so it can pad along. The kitten that is
prevented from walking, fails to develop useful sight.
As does a piglet raised in a very small sty: all it has
seen is concrete walls. On release, it staggers about the
yard bumping into everything – it has to learn to make
use of the visual signals it receives, relating it to the
three dimensional world in which it now finds itself.

At this point in his TED Talk, David Eagleman strips
off his shirt and tosses it into the wings like a strip
dancer, revealing that he is wearing a (very discreet) vest.
Amid applause, he tells us that he is currently linked
to the web and receiving 'likes' on his back in the form
of pressure signals from all over the world, a stroking
sensation unlike any that he has had before. His face
gleams, he looks like a cat purring – proprioception on

tap. And perhaps this is what a cat feels when it is tuned into the stroking hand passing regularly down its spine. Mmmm, the possibilities are endless. I suppose, like all scientific advances, not all of them are positive; it depends what we decide to do with them.

A sobering thought is that beauty is not in the eye of the beholder – but rather, in their brain. The world out there turns out to be a disappointing place – no colour and no sound, simply electromagnetic waves arriving at our eyes (which distinguish between the wavelengths and are interpreted by the brain as colour), and our ears, which pick up the compression and expansion of air and turn them into sounds[46]. The reality we think we know is an illusion, or rather a concoction of our brains. And our brains have evolved in such a way as to make as efficient use as possible of our intake. So if they are wired up differently we may have difficulty interpreting our environment.

We assume that we humans share our sensory experiences but this is not necessarily so. My brother was colour-blind, unable to distinguish between red and green. He only managed to acquire his RAF pilot's licence by listening to the answers given by the man in front of him in the queue, possibly assisted by the fact that there was a desperate shortage of pilots in the early years of the war. A friend was synaesthetic[47]: for him, emotions (and the days of the week), were different colours. While it is quite common to think of anger as red, he knew I did not share the rest of his sensory landscape and kindly made allowances for my inadequacies. Our personal umwelt turns out to be just that, personal. But my brain is my story teller and she/he tells me that my myth is better than your myth.

---

46 Eagleman D Ibid

47 Synaesthesia is a crossover interpretation between any of the senses. For example, taste may be experienced as colour or shape.

The problem that arises in the support of people with disability, particularly those with autism (whose interpretation of sensory experience may be totally chaotic and sometimes painful), is that as carers, we make our judgements and plan our strategies based on our own umwelt, without understanding that theirs is different. It is still not uncommon to place those who are hitting their heads in helmets or arm splints. It may seem strange but people with trigeminal neuralgia, even those who are not on the spectrum, find relief by hitting their heads. Since this pain is not responsive to painkillers, Lindsey Weeks tells us that he would do anything to stop it, 'run in front of a car, bang his head against the wall'[48]. Restraint may prevent impact but does not address the pain that is triggering their self-injury.

To get back to old age: many years ago I attended a disability conference in Canada. The evening floor show was provided by the Graeae Theatre Company. At the conclusion, the actors turned to face the audience and reminded us that many of us would be in wheelchairs and almost all would be disabled in one way or another eventually. Here we were, an audience dedicated to supporting those with disability and we found this salutary. It's different when it is personal.

There are so many things that can go wrong. Starting off with the best intentions, heaving sacks of books from the boot of my car into Oxfam triggered the haemorrhage that dumped debris on my fovea with subsequent sight loss. The world got smaller: overnight shrinkage of umwelt with consequences. One eye has learned to compensate for the other and my long sight is good. Close up is more tricky; finding my glasses is difficult, especially as (never having learned to adapt

---

48 Weeks L (Undated) *A Bridge of Voices*. Documentary audiotape BBC Radio 4 produced by Tom Morton for Sandprint programs.

to varifocals) I now have three pairs, long sight, short sight and bifocal, so I can read and use my screen at the same time (never having learned to touch type). Be patient. In my own mind at least I am beginning to look a little crazy, fumbling in my pockets for the right pair, dropping my stick in the process, leaning forward to pick it up and only just saving myself from overbalancing, since my vestibular system is wobbly.

The brain is constantly in a state of adjusting to curtailment.

It is not only a physical struggle for the ageing to maintain dignity (and in biological terms the fear of being rejected by the tribe). For people with severe autism, their entire lives may be dedicated to the search for coherence, looking for something that has meaning. The brain spends its whole time trying to pick up recognisable patterns, something that makes sense, anything on which it can base its stories. Where it cannot interpret speech, for example, it may recognise the rhythm of the words. So, if a child is echolalic[49], it may respond if we echo back the rhythm of their utterances but be unable to respond if we echo its words. Similarly, they may respond to the pattern of sounds tapped out on the back. It would appear that the electrochemical messages born out of proprioception are more accessible than those born out of the auditory system. This is not really what one might expect, since all messages to the brain come in the same format. Perhaps in this case, the auditory processing area is overwhelmed by hypersensitivity and the pressure processing area is simply providing an alternative route.

When information reaches the brain in the form of electrochemical impulses, it plugs into pathways that are sufficiently similar, so there is confirmation

---

49 'Echolalic' – repetitive speech, either repeating what they have just heard or delayed echolalia repetition of phrases from the past.

through mutual recognition. What is clear is that if we supply signals that are already part of a person's body language, they recognise these, their stress level falls and they calm down.

Pattern recognition is also found in dementia. A friend is in the last days of her life – and although we are close, she doesn't recognise me but lies in bed scratching the sheet. I answer the rhythm of her scratches. Immediately she takes notice, tilts her head towards the sound and listens for more. It was the last time we really met.

Eagleman's vest offers hope, not only to those who are deaf. It may also bring communication and relief from anxiety, even if at a very simple level, to those whose severe disability limits them to pattern recognition. Their need is very great.

Unanswered questions

Technological advances are rampant: it looks as if we shall soon be living in a world so full of drones gathering information that we shall be brushing them off like mosquitoes. And yet, many of the most basic (and interesting) questions about our existence remain unanswered. Are we really the outcome of chance or were we brought into being at the behest of some outside agency? How is it that we can possibly have evolved from the inorganic chemicals that constitute a lump of rock whirling through space, via amorphous plasma to skeletal and sentient beings? Scientists and philosophers are hard at work, chipping away at the unknown, so what follows is a personal tour of the grey areas in my umwelt. It's not enough just to know where I live, I need to know what I am doing here – and what the 'I' is that is doing whatever it is. As well as a reality that turns out to be in itself colourless, are my consciousness and free will an illusion?

I could answer such grandiose questions with a shrug of the shoulders and the – in my lazier moments, rather seductive – catchphrase of a friend's adolescent son when asked to involve himself in any activity – 'Too much "assle"'.

Yes, hassle is laborious and such an attitude certainly simplifies life – we can turn over and go to sleep again. But curiosity is a persistent nagger and keeps on trying to draw back the curtains. I want to know what's going on.

So, while our right brains offer us global impressions, ever since we first crawled out of our caves and started to think about ourselves, our left brains have been hard at work telling us stories that try to make sense of our predicament. We cling to our myths, they protect us from the existential abyss.

To begin with myself, whoever I am, it's difficult to conceive of myself as dead. I cannot use the words 'think of' or 'visualise' since (unless I see myself flapping around in a long white robe clutching a harp, which I don't), there will be no operative sense organs as we know them. Even if I could construct a picture out there, I am so dependent on my boundaries, without feeling, how can me be me? How about the 'me' that feels? Strip off everything, in what sense, if any, does 'I' remain?

What we know for sure at any one time is so fraught with uncertainty. Perhaps it is comforting to reflect that even the greatest of philosophers can get it wrong. Close to hand, I am reminded of the transient nature of understanding by two miniature busts sitting above my desk. The first is a plaster cast bust of that great thinker, Aristotle, in this case an inexplicable one-off rescued from a mass production line of garden gnomes being finished off in an occupational therapy rehabilitation unit. He has not escaped their lurid uniform. His scarlet plinth rests on bottle green grass; his toga is buttercup yellow and skin, geranium pink. Aristotle, who thought the brain was made of phlegm or sperm, which suggests he had not examined either closely, is joined by a plastic replica of Fowler's phrenology cranium, one of an army of bald heads labelled with what were known as 'powers' and 'organs' of the mind. Round the back of his neck a note reads,

'For thirty years I have studied Crania and living heads from all parts of the world and have found in every instance there is a perfect correspondence between the conformation of an individual and his known characteristics. To make my observations available I have prepared a bust of superior form and marked the divisions of the organs in accordance with my researches and varied experience.' LN Fowler

Our world has expanded. What would Aristotle and the great philosophers have accomplished with scanners and rockets and probes? Today the world has unveiled a new neighbour, the planet Pluto – and we can see her face. Not that we didn't know she was there before but until now the best attempts of astronomers could only come up with blurred and pixillated images. After a journey that has taken nine and a half years, 'New Horizon' has arrived at its destination. Having synchronised its path with a fluctuating elliptical orbit, avoided the belt of debris – where a piece of rock the size of a pea could have completely wrecked the mission – and reoriented itself through 90 degrees, the probe is sending back photographs of spectacular beauty and clarity: snowing crystals of nitrogen on ice mountains! In spite of the masculine name (borrowed from Disney), I feel this planet should be referred to as 'she' rather than 'he'. Perhaps this is because planets are like ships afloat on an endless ocean.

Three point six billion miles down here, autumn is in full swing. The wind has an edge, swirls of golden leaves settle on the windscreen: where they have caught the frost, the broad blades of butterbur are shrivelled and charred, as if someone had run a blow-lamp over them.

Looking back, some memories are seminal. Around the age of 16, my sister, who had taught me to read and write and enlightened me on what were known as the 'facts of life', was trying to heave me out of childhood and direct my attention as to what I was going to do once I left school – a subject to which my mind had so far given little attention. I heard myself say, 'I want to know everything'. Rightly, she pointed out that some things are unattainable; this was not going to be possible. But even in my 80s, I still find myself saddled with a voracious if insatiable appetite, not so much for facts as for understanding – what makes us tick?

One day I was discussing our work with Inger Rodbroe, Director of the Danish Institute for Deaf/blind children at Aarlberg. She told me people marvelled at her dedication – but then she turned towards me and said, 'It's the curiosity Phoebe, always the curiosity'. And this is also true for me. I really do want to know what underpins our behaviour. What it is that keeps the human spirit alight even at the boundaries of despair?

No more prevarication – there are still some questions which are difficult to frame, let alone answer. This is partly because, as yet, no plausible resolution has been offered, and partly due to the limitations of my intellect. But I do find it difficult to believe in what I cannot perceive with my senses. At the simplest level, take electricity. I can see what happens when I switch on the light, even wire up a circuit, yet the motivation of the jostling electrons that transmit charge and effect change eludes my grasp. It sounds childish but what is actually happening between negative and positive? What is the invisible pull between deficit and supply? Unless I stick my finger in the socket, my imagination is liable to come to a full stop when I cannot grasp a system with my senses, or devise a satisfactory explanation in my brain.

So should I turn my back on roughly 90% of my experience simply because I cannot visualise the concept? The temptation is to behave like the proverbial ostrich and stick my head in the sand.

While coincidence (the bringing together of unlikely but relevant events) can often be explained statistically, occasionally it is so remarkable it feels as though one has tripped over the edge of the possible into the unknown. Sometimes the link is so bizarre that it does feel as though there is some mysterious 'other' guiding a particular conjunction. Perhaps the most striking incidence in my life was when I was working away from home, in a place where I knew no-one. As a result of an accident, the highly intelligent man I was asked to work with had become totally blind and deaf. Refusing to communicate, he had given up hope and ended up in a unit for people with severe learning difficulties. I thought that perhaps he might be encouraged to speak if he could feel letters instead of speaking words. Fridge magnet letter were too small, I needed large ones that could be recognised immediately – and indestructible since his reactions at that time were entirely negative. I was not sure that my woodworking skills were up to the task. Pondering this, the next day by chance I met a man with whom I had previously had no connection. He said he was a manufacturer. He went on to tell me enthusiastically how he had just bought a machine which could cut out any shape in MDF. I replied that I bet it could not cut out three sets of the alphabet in four inch letters. They arrived within a fortnight. I made racks for them and following the psychologist's advice, the occupational therapist presented them first as 'NO' and 'OK' with the two letters in each case joined by wire. She told me that at first he threw them away and then the penny dropped. He said, 'I've got the 'NO' and I've got the 'OK', where's the 'YES?' While one can talk of synchronicity, such a label brings one no closer to what seems a very far-fetched coming together of demand and supply.

How about telepathy? The evidence for and against wobbles between, on the one hand, passionately held belief in psychic phenomena and, on the other, equally firm rejection by entrenched scientists. Brought up to dismiss the wilder shores of paranormal practice, this doubting Thomas (who nevertheless has personal experience of what can be called 'anomalous processes of energy transfer'[50]), remains unconvinced by the arguments of either camp.

Proof of psychic transmission is hard to come by, partly because of society's scepticism and consequent reluctance to investigate that which appears unlikely and possibly does not exist at all. Scientists, and the rest of us, are unwilling to embark on work that is likely to be lampooned or rejected.

Psychologists reject the 'so called' evidence from psychic research on the grounds that they cannot replicate it. The paranormal camp criticises the papers of the psychologists on the grounds that the statistics they use to analyse their experiments are unsuitable. Myself, I am not convinced that the way experiments set up to test whether or not phenomena such as telepathy are 'real' or imaginary are aimed in the right direction. Let me try and explain what I mean.

I want to start with a story that falls within the category of what is known as dream telepathy. The following story is so deeply personal that the only way I can share it is in the third person.

A woman and her daughter are living on the opposite sides of the world. They have not been in touch with each other for several months. Her daughter has had an operation and the wound has become infected. As the infection spreads, she is in acute pain. During sleep, her mother hears her crying from a great depth, not just anyone crying but her particular voice – she knows at once who it is. From a deep distance, a voice says, 'don't worry, she is not dying but she is in very great pain'. The following day the mother rings her daughter, who confirms the facts of her mother's dream.

---

50 Benn DJ & Honorton C (1994) Does psi exist? Replicable evidence for an anomalous process of energy transfer. *Psychological Bulletin* **115** (1) pp4–18.

This and similar experiences seem to have common features. The first is that they always come out of the blue, they happen, there is no expectation, they are not set up – as in an experiment where there is a 'telepathic sender' and a 'telepathic receiver'. The brain/mind is not anticipating a telepathic event, nor is it necessarily aware of the circumstances surrounding the transmission content – for example, that someone in another room is going to visualise an object and I have to try and perceive what it is. Importantly, the mode of transmission is that of affect rather than intellection. Delivered through feeling, it is most often related to powerfully emotive events. Making a guess as to the subject on a card is not necessarily a suitable starting point for investigating the veracity of affective phenomena. This is not what they are about.

Nevertheless, powerful and valuable as they may be, our insights are not always correct and those of us who are born intuitive need to be wary. We do not seek them. And if they arrive, somehow we have to avoid the lures of projection, introjection and counter transference, together with the temptation to parcel them up with the labels of coincidence, error, fertile imagination, synchronicity and even fraud. If we are aware of these, at least we are pointing ourselves in the right direction. While I cannot reject intuitions and insights, I prefer to observe and allow what happens to happen, rather than get drawn into attempts to instigate or enlarge on them.

And much of what we call intuition does stem from our capacity to read body language with all its subliminal messages, a skill that can be developed if we can learn to empty ourselves of our own agenda. But what of these knowings from afar, when I become aware of extra corporeal happenings beyond my immediate contacts, awareness arriving in what one might term one's 'psychic inbox'?

A sceptic by nature, I am reluctant to embrace 'telepathy'. Nevertheless, in the supporting camp there is some evidence, even if fragile. Studies in dream therapy suggest that sleeping research participants aroused from REM (rapid eye movement) sleep recalled their dreams, and that 'statistically significant' numbers of the dreamers were susceptible to transmitted images from afar[51]. However, Krippner's experiments have been heavily criticised since other investigators have been unable to replicate them[52].

While I am aware that just because an organ appears to be in the right place at the right time does not necessarily imply association – if I were forced to speculate as to where in my body I first become aware of an incoming insight, I should have to point towards the part of the brain known as the periaqueductal gray (PAG). (One has to admit that the PAG has a finger in practically every affective pie but nevertheless it appears to be implicated in where we become aware of our feelings.)

Since all our activities have a feeling tag – even boredom, depending on what question we ask (what do I think about this, or what do I feel about this?) – virtually everything we experience is processed through the PAG's portals. Situated between the forebrain and lower brain stems, it serves as the interface between cognition and affect (as experienced through the activities of the sympathetic nervous system). There is increasing interest in the possibility that the PAG is where we become aware of our selves[53]. And among its multiple

51 Krippner S (2016) *A pilot study in dream telepathy with the Grateful Dead* [online]. Available at: http://stanleykrippner.weebly. com/a-pilot-study-in-dream-telepathy-with-the-grateful-dead.html (accessed April 2016).

52 Alcock J (2005) *Parapsychology, Science or Magic? A psychological perspective*. Oxford: Pergamon Press.

53 Panksepp J (1998) The periconscious substrates of consciousness. In: S Gallagher & G Shear (Eds) *Models of the Self*. Exeter: Imprint Academic.

functions it includes the mechanisms of arousal and control of REM sleep[54].

Standing back, I cherish the word 'inklings', derived from the Middle English verb, 'inkle' meaning to 'utter in an undertone'. These hints from the undermind[55] need to be respected and nurtured but also to be examined with care. They may be immensely valuable insights or red herrings.

So are we more than a box set of conditioned reflexes? I have to believe that I am, not least because of extra-corporeal awarenesses that occasionally come my way. Sceptical, I cannot be sure that these are not imaginings. On the other hand, I cannot deny personal experiences which although they are infrequent, are factual and very specific.

I once, but only once, checked with my apophatic teacher (master in the sense that I was an apprentice) the times and dates when our minds had apparently synchronised. He gave me a very odd look and, in keeping with the negative approach said, 'You are not wrong'. Getting such confirmation was like wringing water from, not just any old stone, but a lump of granite.

Nevertheless, there is always a problem with anecdotal evidence. I cannot prove my experience to you and I have absolutely no explanation to offer at all. Given the random and unexpected nature of these affective perceptions, it is difficult to see how one might set about designing experiments to gather empirical evidence.

With consciousness comes the struggle to find meaning in our lives, to relate ourselves to our environment. What are we doing here? Is our existence accidental? Just something that happened? Our time line is limited and our beliefs or lack of belief sharpens as

---

54 Benattoch EE (2012) Periaqueductal gray: an interface for behavioural control. *Neurology* **78** (3).

55 Claxton G (1998) *Hare Brain Tortoise Mind*. London: Fourth Estate.

we age. Death is an interesting prospect. At a time when both were dying, my husband Peter (a Catholic) and his friend Howard (Marxist and convinced atheist), were talking about their inevitable demise. Howard rightly pointed out that, of the two of them, only he faced the possibility of knowing if he was wrong.

In a vast Catholic church in Tooting, a mother is kneeling in a pew. Her small boy suddenly wails in great distress, 'Mum, God's not here. God's not here'. While it seems plausible that he has confused the priest with the deity, her son has a point – the church is empty. Whatever God is or is not, we cannot see or touch him or her. She or he is not accessible to our normal senses, indeed if this were so, it is unlikely that 'they' would possess the necessary divine attributes – and certainly we do not have the language to encompass these. If we did they would be circumscribed by our human limitations.

What are we talking about when we mention the un-nameable? Are we talking about the same thing? So should you ask me, 'do you believe in God?' I should have to ask you what you mean by God because there are so many different versions. The stance we opt for is to some extent situational. Whether we believe as a Sikh, Hindu, Muslim, Jew, Christian, adopt the slightly more off-line path of Buddhism, opt for a New Age or Pagan, Old Ways or Aquarian point of view, drift along in agnosticism, are a militant atheist or have given up thinking about our place in the universe, seems to depend on the influences we come across or rebel against.

Feet on the ground, dwindling congregations and a Sunday visit to the supermarket suggests that the remnants of faith are rapidly succumbing to 24 hour materialism.

My father was fond of *The Testament of Beauty* by Robert Bridges, chunks of which he taught me. 'We sail a changeful sea, through halcyon days and storm, and when the ship laboureth, our steadfast purpose trembles like as the compass in a binnacle.'[56] Put alternatively, 'Life has its ups and downs and when things get rough we tend to lose our cool'. But even if Bridges' language now sounds old-fashioned, the image of a compass needle trembling in the storm as it seeks to relocate north is evocative.

Up until sudden widowhood, my life had been reasonably predictable: school, university, marriage, family – and then cataclysm. And at that point, my life was trembling, if not on the edge of insanity, at least wobbling around inspecting its perimeter. Broken, I found myself confronting that other great imponderable: God – and the question, is there or isn't there?

Through a series of passive introductions, I found myself being mentored by a Benedictine monk. If this sounds negative, it's apt, since he introduced me to the Apophatic Way, particularly through the work of the Dominican Friar Meister Eckhart.

Eckhart lived in the 13th century and expounded the *via negativa* (as opposed to the Cataphatic way which tries to define God by his/her attributes). Put simply, it is that God may only be known by what he is not. Eckhart's German sermons are simpler to understand than the Latin ones, but even of these he says roughly, 'if you don't understand what I am saying, don't let it bother you'[57]. Nevertheless, even if one cannot always keep up with them, to read his words now is to encounter an authentic voice of wholeness and holiness (one that survives translation from Latin to German and German to English). I do not know any other voice that speaks with such simplicity and authority. No wonder people flocked to hear him.

---

56 Bridges R (1930) *Testament of Beauty,* p1. Oxford University Press.
57 Meister Eckhart (1981) German Sermon 52 pps. 199/203 Classics of Western Spirituality SPCK: London.

Partly as a result of political pressure and partly due to rivalry between the Dominican and Franciscan orders, Eckhart came up against authority who were afraid that, 'he was leading simple and uneducated people into error'[58]. Investigations concerning his teachings were still in process when he died in 1328. He still speaks.

I'm not certain how these theological excursions helped, except to say that over a couple of years my life was changed, I was turned inside out. Rough passage. And if I'm still not sure what it is that I believe, I do find myself in accordance with Carl Jung who, when he was asked if he believed in God, replied that it was more in the nature of knowing rather than belief. This is an interesting distinction and I take it that 'knowing' is used in the sense of 'being aware of', rather than the cognitive process of 'knowing about'.

In the face of all this, how does my case for (an unfashionable, tenuous and increasingly embattled) belief in Christianity hold up in the face of, on the one hand, lack of interest and inertia, and on the other, such astonishing achievements of neurology and cosmologists?

Not all scientists would agree that science and religion are incompatible. The Nobel laureate William Bragg says that science can only make statements about the material world. He suggests that the apparent clash between science and religion derives from Newtonian enlightenment but that the spirit of 20th century quantum enlightenment would see them as complementary. He goes on to say that any apparent opposition resembles the opposition of the thumb and finger on his hand, in the sense that it is an opposition by means of which anything can be grasped[59]. I should

---

58 McGinn B (2001) *The Mystical Thought of Meister Eckhart: The man from whom God hid nothing.* New York: Crossroad-Herder.

59 Tudor Jones G. 16.01.16 Letter to *The Times*.

not like to pretend that I can follow the intricacies of quantum mechanics, but equally I should be reluctant to dismiss the immaterial totally.

The quest for understanding appears to be endless. Every time science thinks it has reached an all-embracing hypothesis, it opens the lid of Pandora's box and out buzzes a whole new swarm of questions. This is particularly true (and again, despite the advances in neuroscience) if we look inwards, especially in terms of affective communication.

In the end (although it is not exclusive to Christianity), I prefer to live with a philosophy that explicitly turns towards my neighbour (thou shalt love thy neighbour as thyself) rather than a free-for-all. I am making a choice, in that I prefer my potential illusion to the possible illusion that it all began somewhere out there before the big bang and will eventually be totally explicable. In spite of my inadequacy, I hang on in.

We are so limited by language: contemplative prayer leads us to the edge of words and abandons us in Presence. This is where I am, not on my own but as part of whatever is. Does this make a difference? For me, yes it does, especially in relation to the work I am engaged in. The ability to empty my brain allows me to focus with intimate attention, not only to what is apparently happening but to the subtext, for example, trauma underlying behaviour. Even bringing 40 years' experience of working with people on the autistic spectrum to bear on a situation, it frequently happens that it's only when I have exhausted my resources and turn away that I become aware of the currents underpinning distress.

So, since there are many other ways of mindfulness, is contemplative prayer more than a way of focus? Actually I don't care, since it works for me and empowers my life and allows me to help others.

At this point there's a knock at my door. I open it. There's no-one about but a small white ghost moth is expiring on the threshold, its waspish abdomen still twitching. Even though its soft head is blunt as a drop-hammer I doubt it could have been responsible for such a loud bang. Fortunately I'm not into omens.

Epilogue

Following the Grand Opening, a headline in the local newspaper[60], 'HOUSING FOR PEOPLE WITH DEMENTIA IS COUNTY FIRST', was greeted by some of its more mentally agile residents with amusement bordering on irritation, depending on their sense of humour. In fact, Limestone View is more important than this. We are a mixed bunch of individuals, where those who have intellectual disabilities or whose minds are beginning to fail, are not separated from either their community or its facilities. The only qualification of residents is that we are old and our bodies are giving us trouble, a situation that if we live long enough will happen to all of us. In some sense we are partners in a social experiment, gentle support and no segregation. Forget the plumbing which is now more or less fixed, what makes Limestone View special is a good idea carried into practice and one that one devoutly hopes will not succumb to governmental cuts in housing benefit.

This morning, a light brush stroke of snow on the hills zigzags up below the scar, picking out a sheep track I've not noticed before. I sit and eat my breakfast watching the sun rise slowly behind the tuft of trees, highlighting successive shoulders.

Very occasionally, something happens that forces one to revise the picture one has of oneself. It's not just a matter of turning over to a new page, but of finding

60 Craven Herald, April 21st, 2016.

oneself reading a different version. Unanticipated, one is not aware of the discrepancy until well into the new book.

A group of poets meet in the town, good poets writing profound and sometimes startlingly beautiful poems, lines that turn the head and images that offer new ways of seeing both the ordinary and the extraordinary. For myself, poetry is something that just happened to me after Peter died; one day it just started to pour out. Blindfold and stumbling, I met and was helped by a number of professional poets but never saw myself as one. 'They' were published, gave readings and sold slim volumes to prove it, I was a hanger-on, the poems I wrote were accidental, cloudy suggestions that slipped out in night when I was still half asleep. And when I found myself accepted by the group and challenged as to why I failed to recognise the gift I had, I came home and looked hard at what I am: scientist, mother, widow, communicator, even writer - but poet? The stranger to herself (has to be third person), spent a restless night until she turned inwards and looked at who she was.

Pronouns are territorial. Switching from 'she' to 'I', defines individuation. Falling asleep, I wake adjusted to seeing myself as a poet.

My left brain has rewritten its story and the balance has shifted. Coincidentally, my raspberry canes have been transplanted from my old house into the communal garden, have taken root both literally and metaphorically and are throwing up new shoots. With a bit of luck we shall be able to share them round next autumn.

Settle is where I live and Bentham is where I used to live. While patience is not my strong suit, I'm beginning to understand that settling in is more than 'getting used to' new people and surroundings but since the backlighting is different, one may have to learn to see and accept oneself from an unfamiliar viewpoint. Above all this change is an organic process that takes time to grow, but one that is facilitated by being friendly and available when need arises, rather than plunged into.

Walking through the town, three people greet me by name. While cringing at the inescapable pun, I am settled in my sheltered flat in Settle. The staff are kind, apart from the bathroom the flat is warm and my neighbours, warm-hearted. If there are ups and downs, they are rooted in persistent physical defects such as buckling vinyl on the kitchen floor, (which will, I hope, eventually be addressed), rather than stragglers from nostalgia. Without complacency, the transition seems to have worked. Here seems a good place to grow old.

And yet, endings are not necessarily tidy. Another telephone call has taken me to see a young man whose autism leads to extreme distress and self-injury. I'm physically and emotionally drained. It is difficult to say no but for the first time I am having to contemplate the end of 'journeyings'. Before crashing out in a seaside hotel, I lean over the rail of the promenade and watch the beach.

It's a Sunday afternoon in early March. Mist muffles the horizon. Tide out, the beach yawns for miles in either direction, North Sea ripples sigh and flop to a standstill on wet sandbanks. The sun is silver, wan, not yet quite sure of its strength - but from push-chair to rollator, the population of the town has turned out en masse. Singles jog, small families meander, infants dibble in the stream, suck their fingers and who knows what sewage, children play chase, dogs bark, horses gallop; a seaside Lowry of pin-figure silhouettes has come alive and is disporting itself.

Twenty miles or so inland is another town, known for its sketch club. Its most famous member is Norman Cornish, a miner at the coalface most of his life. Apart from chronicling the particulars of the ordinary (rows of linen hanging in backyards, men's clubs, women gossiping, a drunk flopped over a rail, men winning coal or climbing gantries, his wife knitting), there is an unflinching watercolour painting on newsprint. So understated it might almost be a smear of grease left on fish-and-chip wrappings, the emaciated figure of Christ hangs from a telegraph pole. Landlines hum round his corpse, irrespective of the burden through which they pass. A life-long Socialist, Norman's intention is clear, a working man spent on the altar of progress. This is not some medieval crucifixion that can be admired and relegated to history but both a political and philosophical question mark. What significance does Christ's self-sacrifice have in today's self-obsessed world? And perhaps more importantly, in the not so remote future of a society directed by human/bionic hybrids or even robots themselves, without inbuilt ethics, or constructed in the minds of designers whose intent is not necessarily benign?

Today is Monday. Waking after a twelve-hour sleep, the beach is empty. The world has gone back to work. The sun is a little stronger: time to drive home.

Philippa brings me an etching for my birthday, an abstract, 'Getting Lost Finding the Maze', inspired by an expedition to locate a maze, while exploring the countryside around Shandy Hall. Although it was created after Lawrence Stern wrote Tristran Shandy, its introspective presence seems so apt that it might well have been part of that book.

Getting Lost on the Way to the Maze

You might think it would be
easy to find,
a sign pointing left,
this way,

or,
two miles to the gentleman's foible.

A maze
lost in tangled lanes,
reflects on its navel,

how shall we know
it's this we've been after
when we chance on the labyrinth
wrapped in enigma?

So often we think we know where we are going and
start off in that general direction, get lost on the way
and find ourselves somewhere completely unexpected.
More questions, more questions. When I stop thinking
about them, then I shall really be old.